Notes on the Old System

Notes
on the Old
System

To
Transform
American
Politics

MARCUS RASKIN
Institute for Policy Studies

DAVID McKAY COMPANY, INC.,   New York

Notes on the Old System

International Standard Book Number: 0-679-50530-X (cloth)
0-679-30266-2 (paper)

LIBRARY OF CONGRESS CATALOG CARD NUMBER: 74-83565
MANUFACTURED IN THE UNITED STATES OF AMERICA

Design by Bob Antler

In memory of my parents
both of whom had a
healthy disrespect for
illegitimate authority

Acknowledgments

In *Notes on the Old System* I am concerned with the obvious. Some of my friends and colleagues have insisted that I make the obvious clear. To the extent I have succeeded it is because of their encouragement. A special debt is owed to Robert Borosage who is a former student, cherished friend, and gifted colleague. I have also had the good fortune of Morris Rubin's comments and suggestions. He is of course the editor and publisher of *The Progressive* magazine. He and his magazine have done much to keep up creative dialogue in public affairs over this generation.

My assistant, Margot White, labored long hours over the manuscript working with me. I also gained much from her trenchant comments. Another brilliant young colleague, Phil Brenner, read and commented on an earlier version of the manuscript, as did Michael Maccoby, who commented with great incisiveness on the relationship between organizational structure and personal character. Len Rodberg also read an earlier version making many useful suggestions as did Richard Barnet, Barbara

Raskin, Joe Turner, Sidney Morgenbesser, and Saul Landau. I was also helped by Tina Smith and Pastell Vann of the Institute for Policy Studies. Thanks are owed also to Edward Artinian and Tren Anderson at David McKay for their devotion to book publishing and political analysis.

Finally I want to thank Noah, Jamin, and Erika Raskin who with Barbara Raskin helped me by playing high politics in the family.

Contents

Notes on the Old System

Introduction

*E*veryone talks about the System. What is the American System? What do we mean by it? What buzz of images do we get when we hear the word "System"? Does it mean our three branches of government, each working together and against one another for the public good? Does the System mean a way of governing which assures that the weak will remain weak and the strong become stronger? Is it, therefore, the development of a series of legal, administrative, and property arrangements that protect the strong against the weak? Is the System a hodgepodge of national security bureaucracies and economic baronies held together through presidential authority? Is the System a new branch of government called the Presidency? Is the System a shorthand for capitalism in which the rich, the quick, the clever, the unseen, set out paths which the wretched and mystified must travel? Is the System a way of life that rewards people like Richard Nixon? Can the System be changed?

These Notes are an attempt to describe some of the workings of the American System. They are in no way meant to be definitive. They may be useful to the reader and the student in seeing relationships for what they really are. Or a fact or two may take on a new significance in the way I have related that fact to others.

Finally, these Notes are an appeal from a man who is appalled and angry, who has seen the moral, political, intellectual (but not economic) bankruptcy of our "brightest and best"; the development of national security, defense, and economic institutions that have taken on Frankenstein qualities; a succession of Presidents who believed that they embodied the general will separate from the people; and a Congress caught in a purgatory divorced both from power and from the citizenry. The people sit appalled in front of a stage (television set) of dancing picaros, mountebanks, sadists, and fools in Brooks Brothers clothes.

So I suppose that these Notes are an appeal to the American audience to leave their seats and become the actors of history. Otherwise, they will remain objects and pawns of leaders and faulty institutions. Life is difficult enough, with people facing their own personal tragedies. It is not necessary to heap on people the crazed ideas of the few, the institutional madness structured as rationality, and the domination by forces that are destructive and genocidal. Can we begin the task of transforming the life of the society into many societies, into a politics of rebonding? Can we free ourselves from the metallic, technochronic dead hand which may leave us with the terrifying choice of mass zombie-ism or extermination?

There are a few governing principles of American political life that I hope the reader will keep in mind when he reads this book. These principles reflect themselves in the modern organization of the state structure which includes not only the government, but also schools, armed forces, financial institutions, and industrial corporations. One principle is that everything in the American empire is for sale; indeed, *should* be bought and sold. Operators of the economic system do not necessarily see it as either idiosyncratic, "unethical," or strange that the law itself should be considered a commodity that can be bought and sold. If the exchange principle applies to labor and its products generally, and to other human interactions, objects, and processes in life, it is hardly a giant step to assume that the law, lawyers, lobbyists, and politicians are for rent and sale. Those who try to "make it" in the political economy as entrepreneurs, managers, or owners come to believe in the centrality of the profit motive in all social institutions and interactions.

The contradiction is that most people do not want to sell or rent others. They are appalled by such a relationship and sickened by its implications for law and society. Yet, they are caught in a web of roles and functions in which they use others and are used by them. In the process, they repress their natural decency and learn to curb their standards, expectations, and outrage.

A second governing principle asserts that people are innately selfish and individualistic. Selfishness, according to Anglo-American empiricists, is a reflection of man's inherent nature and is the fundamental justification for the existence of the state. The state is seen as providing the people with a structure beyond themselves which will contain their selfish natures through law and force. The modern liberal state takes into account man's predilection toward degeneracy, granting people their lusts, but always seeking to protect them from themselves and others (whether at home or abroad).

Leaders of states assume that the people are neither perfect nor perfectible. Therefore, politics, laws and their enforcement are not matters for the people but for the "responsible" few. As a result, laws inevitably are used against particular groups and

classes to maintain order and stability in the nation. The contradiction to this principle arises when the people, however individuated or alienated, begin to question the authority and judgment
of the few. Demands are then made for freedom by the many.
They resent the lusts of the few which are masked as liberties.

The third principle of politics is derived from a much older
assumption. It has been posited that the state should aim at the
"general good" and express that good to a greater degree than any
separate group or institution within the state. Thus, whether or
not statesmen want the role, the state has, by its nature, the
mandate to act as "moral legislator" for all its citizens.

The fundamental question, of course, was who would act as
legislator for the state? Some assumed that the natural form
would be a democracy in which all citizens would decide and
define the laws. Others believed in a republic, in which elected
citizens would act as legislators. The question was crucial because
if one assumed that the state would act for the common good, it
would be endowed with great power and would accept few limits
on its actions. Even toward the individual citizen, its powers
would be great, for it would claim to be acting both in the "public
interest" and in the individual's "true" interest.

In the modern-day United States, neither a democracy nor a
republic exists in operation. The state helps the powerful. The
emergence of large-scale armed forces and corporate capitalism
colonizes people into huge organizational structures. They are
then assumed to have only abstract interests, which can be
represented through barons, the leading managers and owners of
the bureaucratic structures. This form of organization—the cor-
porative form—is perhaps the most pervasive form of the modern
state in the world. The pretension of acting as moral legislator has
not been abandoned, however. As a result, the state assumes great
power and with the corporations organizes the attitudes and
operational beliefs that reinforce the individual's loneliness and

sense of helplessness. Massive propaganda and advertising are devoted to deflecting any personal or political consciousness which might lead to independent and purposeful actions. The person disappears in this framework, as does any opportunity for the people to act cooperatively (as citizens) toward common ends. The ability of citizens to present, deliberate, and exercise control, as well as set limits and make their own mistakes, has been whittled and splintered away.

The contradiction to this principle is that the people still expect the state to act according to its own rhetoric, to promote "the pursuit of happiness" and "the general welfare" as expressed in the Preamble to the Constitution. As a result, when the ugliness and corruption of the corporate form are revealed, people feel soiled and betrayed. They seek a return to the original notions of this principle, demanding higher levels of participation.

These three principles of governing are a handbook for tyranny. Modern tyranny is the maintenance of organized power in the hands of the state, its military and bureaucratic apparatus, and its corporate system. The corporate forms seek the death of politics, favoring instead hierarchic and administrative processes through which human concerns are transformed into matters of interest, ideological pretension, or quantitative measurement. Deliberative bodies such as the Congress or the town meeting are seen as outmoded. Indeed, many members of Congress prefer to support oligarchy, imperialism, and administrative managerialism, favoring decision-making procedures that cannot be seen or heard, only felt. Thus, as I will suggest, the Congress has followed other deliberative forms into decline and triviality to the extent that it has denied its roots in the people.

The doctrinal books on the American form of government seldom discuss these matters, preferring to discuss "balanced government," checks and balances, or the importance of "protecting the Presidency." As we sit horrified at the drama and farce in Nixon's Watergate, however, we can no longer accept these outmoded perspectives. The System has become a luxury the people can no longer afford. They can "afford" one another in assemblies and juries with a return of the power of deliberation and execution to themselves. Nor, for that matter, can we accept a political science which fits comfortably into that system.

1 / The President's Burlesque and His Bank of Political Power

A President's cloak of legitimacy is woven from the fabric of responsibility for political stability and unity (United) and for imperial expansion (States). A President believes that being concerned with these responsibilities is the very meaning of the law and the Constitution. He is taught this lesson by no less a mentor than Abraham Lincoln. So long as a President accepts the principle of unity and imperial expansion, and appears to fulfill this principle, no government official would ever be willing, according to former Justice Tom Clark, "to question the President's assertion that what he was about to do was constitutional." This mode of wielding power is called *Constitutionalism.*

A presidential aspirant who knows his place will mask his own appetites and the appetites of those around him with the rhetoric of stability and unity. Obviously the appetites of individual Presidents differ. For example, five-star General Eisenhower, having been satiated with his wartime experiences as commander-in-chief of the Allied Forces in Europe, came to the Presidency with a modest appetite for bellicosity and war. On the other hand, ex-navy lieutenant Kennedy had a larger appetite requiring more political capital, more power. He wanted to "get things moving again," "to pay any price," take up any "burden." The more capital a President needs, the more tattered the cloak of Constitutionalism becomes.

A President does not carry the Constitution in his back pocket. He is command and result oriented: "Get me this," "Do this," "Do that." Command power wielded within a constitutional framework is understood operationally by a President to mean the limits placed on him by representatives of independent power, the "barons"—men who control or manage the banks, the insurance companies, the armed forces, large industrial corporations, bureaucracies, and labor unions. These men and groups represent real class forces within the society, and potential threats to him personally. A President sees the various groupings of American society as "audiences" controlled by directors who are offstage. He believes that governing is carried out in private, either among the bankers in the board rooms, the military in the war game rooms, or the corporate leaders in private clubs. He is applauded and respected by people who are recognized as "winners." They are the only ones he talks "with" rather than "at" and whom he respects rather than patronizes.

In his official capacity, the President is like a Golem: he is the instrument of those groups, leaderships, and classes that guide the American destiny; and he is at other times their master, accumulating to himself and the Office great dependencies. If he is astute, the President may expect and receive sympathetic hearings for his adventures from the assorted leaderships because they have used similar means in pursuit of power, and have practiced similar methods in obtaining and retaining that power.

They understand the nature of politics in like ways and have a shared consciousness of what the American System has become.

This interplay between presidential power and independent sources of power affects every aspect of the Presidency. For example, institutional leaders expect Presidents to appoint individuals from within their own high ranks to positions of corresponding rank and power in the bureaucracy. It is assumed that representatives from defense industries will be appointed to run the Department of Defense. (For example, Nixon appointed David Packard, head of Hewlett-Packard, one of the leading defense contractors, to be deputy secretary of defense.)

On the other hand, the institutional leaders expect a President to appoint his "own" retainers to high positions around him. They accept the idea that a President may either elevate or submerge the ambitious and the careerist among his appointments, in exchange for their obedience and loyalty. A President's coterie, including the senior civil servants who occupy the Executive Office of the President, are adequately rewarded through pay and privilege. Every President attempts to control his retinue's appetite for personal gain and glory by promising them a greater future if they represent him than if they become brokers either for various "outside" interests or for their own economic interests and adventures. The President's men are to defer their own interests until they have left government "service." If they are judicious and careful, showing that they know how to serve the President without undercutting the power of major institutions, they will have succeeded in helping the President and the System. For such service, a prudent adviser will help such a member of his retinue obtain new status outside the government. For example, Lyndon Johnson's "valuable hunk of humanity," Jack Valenti, operated as a speech writer and valet for Johnson before becoming president of the Motion Picture Producers Association.

Advisers to strong Presidents learn how to remain silent and be circumspect. They will not speak on all issues even if asked. In this way, they "conserve credit points," supposedly gaining them greater leverage on issues with which they are concerned. Since most issues that come to the attention of a White House staffer and the President are fraught with moral and political consequences, advisers who are silent about their value judgments very quickly turn themselves into operators who can be used by the President or senior members of the administration for any purpose. By their silence, they show that they are "good soldiers," having no morals or politics of their own as barriers against rotten or grotesque actions. Their loyalty is to the President, and such loyalty is deemed necessary to the wielding of presidential power, to the Presidency itself.

The barons, leaders of organized and powerful institutions, look to presidential power and to the President as a mediator between them. However, they also see the President as an authority symbol that reinforces their own legitimacy and their right to hold power. They do not expect him or his coterie to undermine their autonomy or challenge their pecking order by choosing, or causing to be chosen, the leadership of their own constituencies. Thus, President Nixon erred when he meddled in the presidential politics of the Teamsters Union, first granting a pardon to James Hoffa but then denying him the right to challenge his chair warmer, Frank Fitzsimmons, as a condition of Hoffa's parole.* The barons of these organized power groups expect the President to provide the kind of brokering leadership that will maintain an empire abroad and order among the economic classes at home. He is expected to present to the passive branches—the Congress, the courts, the media, and the American audience generally—policies that have already been legitimated

---

* It is to be noted that Nixon should have curtailed Charles Colson's appetites. When Colson left the White House and ceased to be Nixon's counsel, he took the Teamsters on as his new client.

informally outside the public forums by means of baronial agreements. A President also has a sales function. The industrial barons expect the leadership of the state to promote the life (profitability) of consumer goods as President Nixon did when he proclaimed that it was *Everyman's* patriotic duty to buy American cars.

If a President is politically adept, he will be designated the Unifier and will be anointed to present the appearance of national unity to the nation (the people and the apparatus) and to the world. Once a President is so anointed, the leadership of the quasi-autonomous baronies—whether "inside" or "outside" the state apparatus—will support virtually any presidential policy, provided he acts decisively. It is not necessary that a crisis exist for a President to act. It is enough that a crisis is *perceived* to exist. It will then be talked about as if it exists in fact, and presidential action will be assessed within a "crisis" framework.

A President is expected to explain to the people the benefit of any independent "crisis" action he has taken. He may declare that there is no other choice, or that a particular choice was taken to preserve the System itself. Thus, modern war and imperialism may be explained as defending democracy or free enterprise, use of the national security apparatus is "justified" as protection of the homeland against foreigners and bureaucrats who are invariably making or getting into trouble, and tax benefits to the rich are rationalized as necessary so that the rich will be able to profit and "invest" enough for the poor to benefit.*

On the other hand, where the organized interest groups or the barons find that they are suffering material damage and where they are unable to identify the President's unity theme with their

---

* Even if a particular presidential policy fails to accomplish its stated objective, it is likely that merely by *acting,* a President will have greatly increased Executive power and decreased the space of the citizenry. The citizenry, who see their own space already whittled away by the barons and corporations, may therefore not protest.

own interests, they will demand personal attention and special explanations from him. If a President believes it unnecessary to explain his actions to the people and to the barons of the institutions, he may pay dearly for this "error." He may find himself isolated and reduced to the appearance and ornaments of power. This may mean that even a conservative President will be isolated, having "no troops but the troops" upon whom to depend. If he finds himself in such a situation, a President may shore up his legitimacy by using military forces—as Herbert Hoover did in 1932, dispersing the unemployed bonus marchers with regular army forces under the command of Douglas MacArthur and his deputy, Dwight Eisenhower.

As a rule, Presidents play on people's fears and supposed need for order and quiet. Politicians and businessmen believe that people would much prefer order than freedom, the latter a commodity of use only to the young. Presidents since Franklin Roosevelt have seen their task as one of deciding between painful choices or, to put the matter another way, as one of distributing pain. The technique of distribution adopted, and its success or failure, will determine whether the distributor is viewed by his audience and his objects as a virtuoso or a fool. Thus, if a President can give pleasure through pain, he will be viewed as a master of statecraft. For example, if a President can *prepare* for war, thereby securing employment, food, and shelter (that is, pleasure) for the audience, without actually going to war (pain) or changing the class structure, he will be hailed as a master and peacemaker.

If the President is of a conservative bent and of lowly station, he will accept the hierarchic order as it is. He will define the American dream in modest terms: that which the people already have will not be taken from them. He will say that politicians should raise no false expectations since there will be no change in the class structure of the society. He will guarantee that those who have possessions and illusions will not have them taken away by those who prefer another set of public illusions. In exchange, such an aspirant will expect loyalty and submissiveness from the people who exist in lonely and individuated lives. He will use force and, when necessary, adventure to ensure such submissiveness. With even passive acquiescence from the people, a President will declare this as evidence of their support and will barter such support with organized power: the elites of the military, the corporations, even the churches. Such elites will honor "a man of the people" if he can be trusted to ensure that the people remain privatized and immobile. A President who masters the mode of governing as distributor and unifier can expect cooperation from the rich if he courts their power, while playing on their paranoia and their fear that the unorganized will take away their property and their "way of life."

To sustain the support of the leaders of organized groups, politicians as a general rule spend a great deal of their time in "touching base." Such activity for the most part is symbolic. For example, the politician makes it his business to be "seen" with certain people and at certain events. Often what is said at such events is secondary to simply being present. Politicians believe that touching base reflects a healthy respect for the hierarchic structure of the society, as it is. It explores, in various ways, the power of the barons at the top of the pyramid. Presidents who have a conventional view of the office touch base only with the largest and most powerful constituencies, except when a purely symbolic point is being made for the mass of the population. A conventional President, for example, accords symbolic recognition to various elements in American life merely by being photographed with them. He may be pictured talking to veterans, office workers, cripples, or coal miners. No substantive conversation will be held with such people unless they are organized. If they are organized, conversations will be held only with their leaders.

Presidential parades serve an important legitimating function for a President, besides giving him a warm inner glow. He has an opportunity to be seen and to "press the flesh," as Lyndon Johnson put it. Abroad, parades have more complex purposes. When a President is "well received" in a foreign country—cheered by crowds of its citizens—he knows that he has the support of that country's leadership since it is assumed that there would be no other way the masses would come forward to cheer a foreign leader. A President can further conclude that this is evidence of the "stability" of the foreign country because such large masses of the population can be organized and directed for such a purpose at the command of the state. If the crowds are large, it will then appear to the American people through international satellite communications that their President is a world leader of whom they should be proud and, therefore, should refrain from criticizing.

The modern managers of the American state, including presidential aspirants, do not see themselves as tyrants. They see themselves as symphony conductors—this time cueing in the violins, next time the horns, but always trying to control the delicate balance which is to be struck between repression and tolerance, appearance and fact. While they do not ride white horses into battle, they do not shirk from bloodshed—as was made clear, for example, by Nelson Rockefeller during the Attica prison rebellion, or as William Howard Taft told his wife during the 1895 Pullman strike: "It will be necessary for the military to kill some of the mob before the trouble can be stayed. They have killed only six yet. This is hardly enough to make an impression." [1] Modern Presidents, even if they do not personally lead the charges, attempt to exercise control over the forces of violence with complex technological devices. Using the most sophisticated communications technology, in 1965 President Johnson followed the battle through Santo Domingo block by block, releasing platoon sized groups to proceed from one street corner to the next. Frequently, from the middle 1960's until the present, the bombing war in Southeast Asia has literally been commanded from the White House where at times not only targets were chosen, but aircraft types, bomb loads, times over target, and restrikes were specified in detail.[2]

In America, leaders are respected for being, or appearing to be, "self-made." The "self-made" are seen as lonely scufflers who fight their own way to the top, bringing only themselves and, if necessary, their retainers, along with them. Even John Kennedy was pictured as someone "afflicted" and "burdened" by wealth and position which he had to "overcome." The self-made man may be applauded for his anger, as in the case of George Wallace; noticed for his slyness, as in the case of John Connally; or chosen for his apparent foolishness, as in the case of Gerald Ford. All must be prepared to show a way to control the populace and keep the empire. Whether patrician or bureaucrat, such a conventional Presidential aspirant must accept the American empire as *the* definition of unity. This means that he must make his peace with militarism. He must not undercut military power, either the $100 billion a year imperial war budget, the 13.5 million people who are on veterans' pensions, the defense contracting system, or the 5.5 million people employed through the Department of Defense as uniformed or civilian workers. As the novelist from South Carolina, William Simms, wrote to his senator in 1847:

> You must not dilate against military glory. War is the greatest element of modern civilization, and our destiny is conquest. Indeed, the moment a nation ceases to extend its sway it falls a prey to an inferior but more energetic neighbor.[3]

(As we shall see when we discuss Senator Barry Goldwater's position, we will find that Simms' ideology held sway in Congress throughout most of the twentieth century.)

A conventional President recognizes and seeks ways to implement a business-government "partnership." He accepts the principle that the largest units of economic life must be organized as profit-seeking ventures which require direct and indirect state subsidy. In his role as politician and vote getter a President will take into account the suburban country club set, knowing that their economic liabilities are great, their psychological vulnerability immense, and their need to be publicly "stroked" insatiable. The System's President must be cognizant of different kinds of bureaucrats. He must distinguish between those who merely seek employment, security, and pension, as against those who enjoy manipulation and control which is exercised in the higher reaches of the bureaucracy—where millions of people become "problems" reified by statistics and abstract categories. Finally, the conventional President and the conventional candidate within the System must be prepared to support the labor movement so long as it does not organize the entire working class, accepts the principle of higher productivity related to higher wages, and sees itself as a symbiotic complement to the capitalist system.

This style of wielding presidential power is relatively modest. The President undertakes to broker the various large corporations, the largest banks, the military bureaucracies, and the public and private baronies serving them, protecting them, and then skimming off a small percentage of "interest." This interest might be called "bankable" power, or credit. "Bankable" power is the reserve power that a President and his retinue may spend for personal glory, silliness, adventure, or fashion disguised as *program*. Presidential tradition is part of this "bank," and great Presidents are viewed as ones who accumulated large amounts of power to the presidential bank for future use. As noted, Presidents are able to add greatly to the presidential bank of power if they justify their actions and program on the basis of promoting internal stability and unity. This style of governing is known as "consensus politics," or governing *for* the System. The "activist" President is the one who adds most to the presidential bank of power. Since Franklin Roosevelt, Presidents have been encouraged by the liberal-minded to develop a fourth branch of government, the Presidency.

Some Presidents may not wish to govern by consensus, preferring instead to rule by force of personality, or by direct and indirect forms of repression. Even so, they remain obliged to cloak their actions in legitimate forms. This is not very onerous. As we shall discuss, there is much precedent to draw upon from the tradition of the Executive and the delegation of emergency and martial-law powers to him. If, like Woodrow Wilson and Franklin Roosevelt, he is able to affect an appearance of incorruptibility, he will more easily be able to enforce internal security measures without significant cruelty or dissent.* He can rely on the total obedience of the officer corps of the armed forces and on the bureaucracy. For a time he may expect to have the allegiance of those in the declining working middle classes who seek their identity by protecting their mortgaged property, unserviceable consumer goods, and what little they have earned.

---

* Authoritarians must be personally incorruptible—at least, they must have the power and acumen to turn their corruption into the kind of privilege which everyone in the society comes to recognize and automatically accept by virtue of their acknowledged status. Thus, corporate executives are given perquisites through the tax laws; generals are given soldiers to clear their lawns; wardens are given prisoners as their servants; and high government officials, whether socialist or capitalist, are given palaces and dachas to use. Such social practices become intertwined with the meaning of authority itself, like the orb and scepter of monarchy. It is crucial that such privileges are seen as part of legitimate (lawful) authority and accepted as customary by the people. Indeed, it is even better if they can be taught to think that such privileges are within their own reach. If those in authority do not know how to wear this mode of corruption unpretentiously, they will be attacked unmercifully.

An activist President (and those operating with his aura) sees himself *outside* the System: laws which are made through him do not apply to him and the principles of behavior expected of most citizens are not expected of him or of the barons. The activist President sees his goals as those which his nation should have. He borrows ideas and methods on how to lead from totalitarians as well as democrats. The activist President, one who has style and nerve, is able to channel the bureaucracy according to principles that he fashions, provided he follows certain customs and does not attempt to undercut its status. He works with the groups as they are, hoping through this method to coopt them in the direction he wants. Modern emphasis on planning means that the activist President uses the White House staff, the staff of the Presidency, the staffs of the huge corporations, the military, and the police to develop detailed projections of the society. Depending on his ideological cast, he will decide whether this planning function should be concentrated within his immediate retinue, in the entire bureaucracy or in corporate-military and bureaucratic committees of the Executive Office.*

The President who tries to fill all the spaces with his own will is hampered by a bureaucracy which sees itself as the "permanent" government. As Hans Morgenthau has pointed out:

> When we refer to the executive branch of the government, we are really making use of a figure of speech in order to designate a multiplicity of varied and more or less autonomous agencies that have but one quality in common: their authority has been delegated to them either by the President or by Congress. But neither the President nor Congress is able to control them.[4]

* The largest office of the Executive Office of the President is the Office of Management and Budget (OMB) which formulates "objectives and objective" legislation as well as long-term program goals. It also controls the budget for the President.

Nevertheless, the executive branch attempts to speak through the President and he through it. It is the task of the Executive Office of the President, including the Office of Management and Budget, to standardize the words used by the Executive, at least on matters of legislation and budget—except in the area of national security.

Career officials believe that they serve "the Presidency rather than the President." An activist President, however, can use this rhetoric to enlarge his own power and that of the Office at the expense of other parts of the government since career officials will assume that the need to increase the presidential prerogative over all aspects of government—and possibly of the society—is beyond question. Only those Presidents who attempt to decrease the presidential prerogative, or who have not learned how to make their corruption appear as privilege, will be criticized by the bureaucracy of the executive building.

A moment of political horror occurs when the obedience structure fails within the bureaucracy. When it is made public that an irreparable split exists between the executive branch bureaucracies and the President's White House Executive Offices (in other words, between the "permanent" government and the "tenant" at the White House), the President becomes a "pitiful, helpless giant." When a cloud hovers over the head of a President, the headless bureaucracy increases its own power, using such language as "rule of law," "consistency," and "administrative guidelines" as a way to keep the ship of state afloat and the status of bureaucracy intact.

The authority of government usually means paternalism. The father is the government symbolized in the Presidency, and the children are the governed. The "father" aims at the proper good of the governed—"proper good" being defined by his good judgment. What is "best" for the governed is determined by the President who holds office through election or selection. He is given tools for mature judgment through a variety of instruments, institutions, and perquisites which include patronage, intelligence gathering, emergency powers, media domination, and bureaucracy. Yet, as even the cleverest fathers know, total power, whether stemming from persuasion or terror, is never obtained over children. Those with authority, even Presidents, soon learn that neither individuals nor institutions bend easily to their will, even in response to a hard ideology of sacrifice accompanied by direct and indirect forms of terror. Even the "good" leader, when acting as moral legislator for the people, will discover the limits of authority and paternalism. Any attempt by one or a few to assert authority over the many (oligarchic authority) can degenerate into raw power when it attempts to maintain itself against challenges. At that point, the assertion of raw power will blot out the spaces for the individual and his natural associations.

People hesitate to apply their own good sense and natural purpose to political action because they come to believe that they will become beasts unless awesome power, cleverly arranged through the state apparatus, will force people to be "good." Richard Nixon hoped to be a modern Solon. He hoped to present to the people a new moral code. But the communicators, the universities, schools, and national media, did not share Nixon's moral teachings. He believed that those who had been in charge of the civic and moral teachings of the society, the eastern establishment, had lost their way and their will to govern. In his view they were morally permissive. Nixon, Spiro Agnew, and other members of the Nixon group believed that the eastern *male* establishment was frightened of its wives and children, two hitherto silent classes which had made a terrible fuss about the Indochina war. The trap for the Nixon administration, as we shall discuss, was that the law and order its members professed and proclaimed, the moral lessons it wanted to teach, fell entirely within the substance and "ethic" of capitalism: like everything else, law and order were for sale. And if not for sale, then for rent, as they were themselves.

There is another mode of governing in which a President might seek to change the relationship between the classes through income, wealth, and power redistribution. To do so, he must first appeal to the "beneficent" impulses of the rich, demystify the geometry of corporate ownership, call forth biblical incantations from Deuteronomy, and point out the obvious contradictions between those who work for little or nothing and those who are rewarded for doing little or nothing as their work. He must then embarrass and humiliate the rich, playing on their inner fears, sense of guilt, and their own cònfusion about their intrinsic worth. And he must make pleas to their children who might support his actions because of their natural benevolent impulses. He must exhort the employed classes, telling them that they should have a say in what is made in the factories and sold in the marketplace. He must appeal to the consumers on the same grounds, suggesting ways in which the various groups could develop their own economic forums for this purpose. If he travels this road, such a President must be prepared to live unostentatiously, neither as an ascetic nor a profligate. He must eschew the ornaments of power, knowing that such ornaments are offensive to enemies and friends alike. If a President seeks to act in the name of the poor and the working class, however, he must still use all the power that has been legally put into his hands, including emergency power, reiterating the principle that necessity must govern the actions of Presidents for the good of the greatest number.

Needless to say, a President committed to the latter goals would find himself doing battle with capitalism and imperialism. He would be required, therefore, to fashion a new set of symbols from the American landscape of myths and dreams which would cause direct confrontation with the bloated genocide-preparing military system. Given his purpose of promising full economic and political citizenship, and assuming that such a President had consummate political skill, it is likely that he would still find himself in deep personal trouble—courting regicide. If he were less than consummate in his methods and, like a demogogue, saw himself as a leader *of* the people rather than *from* the people, it is likely that he would not engender support for his activities and his stewardship would degenerate. In such a case, it is likely that the organs of legitimated violence—the prisons, police, armed forces, schools, factories, and hierarchic power itself—would remain untouched.

Antonio Gramsci has said that the myth-prince, the kind of President I have just described,

> cannot be a real person, a concrete individual. It can only be an organism, a complex element of society in which a collective will, which has already been recognized and has to some extent asserted itself in action, begins to take concrete form.[5]

Gramsci had in mind a political party, one which itself could challenge the industrial, military, and bureaucratic elites and their hegemony. I have discussed the issue of a new political party elsewhere. The question remains whether a political party can now reflect collective reason and reasonableness without prior participatory action: action that requires sustained public discussion, citizen planning for plausible alternatives, and the mobilization of local power to carry out the results of the public discussion. What is *not* likely, however, is that a President with such a set of purposes would in the present System even be able to obtain power.

The American two-party system is a strainer, and a President comes to power because he is a man who knows how and with whom, as members of Congress say, to "cut a deal." He must not offend certain institutional groups which believe they are the System. While they do not have to agree with a President on every issue, they must be neutralized—made to feel that there is no threat to their interests, but merely some adjustments which they might have to make. Thus, for example, the southern plantation owners feared John Kennedy because of his preachments on civil rights. He assuaged the plantation owners with vast agricultural benefits for mechanizing their farms, replacing black workers with machines, and increasing benefits to the owners for not growing food. Lyndon Johnson was a master at managing bills through the Senate which were thought of as reforms, but whose fine print left the major institutional forces of the society un-touched, or even greatly reinforced. Appropriations for Great Society programs seemed designed to help the wretched but turned out in practice to meet the needs of the "helpers," the bureaucracy and the middle class and the rich. As Douglas Dillon, Treasury secretary for both Kennedy and Johnson—and scion of his own investment banking firm—put it: "the rate of increase of spending for arms, space and interest on the national debt was double that of the Eisenhower Administration while the Kennedy Administration spent one third less on programs other than na-tional security."[6]

Both Kennedy and Johnson were thought of as liberal, activ-ist Presidents who did the bidding of the liberal and reform wing of the Democratic party. The reformers, however, have had a confused ideology. They have invariably pinned their hopes on a national leader who would emerge with a "good" national pro-gram to make the System "work." In the last generation, until 1972, liberals no longer questioned the maximization of private wealth, or the principle that advertising should manipulate the demand for consumer goods, or the hegemony of monopoly business and state power as the bedrock of American society. From the end of the Second World War, liberals provided the music for the corporations and asserted the need for a strong national leader who would operate benevolently through rhetoric and the bureaucracy for the common good of the System. His powers would verge on the dictatorial.

Benevolent dictators, always fashionable in times of crisis, overturn representative or participatory bodies. They leave behind them a strengthened state apparatus and the wreckage of a colonized people who are setups for ordinary dictators. Theodore Roosevelt's stewardship theory of government is the American form of the benevolent dictator. He is to play an active role to keep the System going, especially its economic underpinnings and ideology. In his autobiography Theodore Roosevelt said that the President "was a steward of the people bound actively and affirmatively to do all he could for the people. . . . I declined to adopt the view that what was imperatively necessary for the nation could not be done by the President unless he could find specific authorization for it." Roosevelt believed that "the Executive power was limited only by specific restrictions and prohibitions appearing in the Constitution or imposed by Congress under the Constitutional power." [7]

Roosevelt recognized the importance of setting standards in the society which would show the difference between the "good" capitalist and the "bad" capitalist. It was the task of the President to differentiate between the two, thus diffusing the anger of the people against the entire economic system. In a profound sense, Theodore Roosevelt believed that a President's purpose was to obtain the people's loyalty to the capitalist system. The most respected Wall Street lawyer of his time, and a former secretary of state, Elihu Root, applauded Theodore Roosevelt by saying to his clients and friends that Roosevelt was "the greatest conservative for the protection of property and capital in the city of Washington." [8]

President Franklin Roosevelt, during his term of office, gave further development to the stewardship theory in practice. He and his advisers believed that the Great Depression required the President to fill all the public spaces so that a broken, frightened people would not overthrow the capitalist system. Congress and the Supreme Court were passive institutions which could not begin to act for that purpose. It had long been the case that the American people, psychologically, could not identify with the 535 people in Congress and a Supreme Court that appeared abstruse and remote. Furthermore, the courts were protecting the principle of the negative state—limiting the scope of legislation and governmental power to controlling the excesses of capitalism. On the other hand, the President had come to be seen by all as the supreme actor—in both senses: he could move things and people, and he could feign their movement. He was the modern magician who could deal with the "economic royalists." Economically, the nation had been organized by huge corporations that did not respect either state or local law.[9] Social reformers believed that there was not enough "power," expertise, or indeed, honesty on the local level either to work with or to control the modern corporation.* Congress was seen as merely representative of such "local" interests. It was small time, somewhat irrational, eccentric, and a bit funky. In any case, it was not an institution that could "responsibly" (that is, through a clearly articulated ruling-class

---

* It should be recalled that corporate charters were at one time given only for limited time and limited purposes. Twenty years was given for the corporateers as their time to "make good." The New York state constitution at one point in the nineteenth century required a two-thirds vote of both houses before a charter could be granted. And in most states, even until the twentieth century, the size of corporations was limited.

position) manage the life of the nation or "control" the corporations.

From this situation, several doctrines were developed ex post facto to justify the principle that a President had a bottomless well of residual powers in the White House. One such doctrine was based on the belief that the government, the state's operational embodiment, was to care for the general welfare. And once the corporation was unleashed, the only means which anyone but an anarchist saw to carry out the general welfare was through the existence of a strong, centralized, executive sovereign in all its pretension and scope.

From the latter part of the nineteenth century, it was taken for granted by virtually all social reformers that since the state helped to foster the growth of material production, it therefore had legitimate claims on such production and should have access to its profits. The reformers believed that the state's positive role was to determine the public interest in the clashes between capital and labor. It was to "enforce those measures which will assist in realizing all the conditions of a sound industrial system against both the greed of capitalists and the short sightedness of the laborer." [10] The state bureaucracy, using modern social science techniques, the work ethics of the social gospel, and watered down socialism, was to become an instrument to protect the natural resources and to develop a rational economic system as well. [11]

State governments were seen as the "laboratories" for new ideas and reforms. Wisconsin, for example, at the beginning of the twentieth century seemed to offer hope—since crushed—that state governments would be able to operate independently and actively without interference from the great corporations. Progressives who had operated at the local and state level in this way believed that the federal government as well could challenge the corporations to operate in a positive way. They believed that the state could be more than a dump truck which merely picked up the broken bodies and lost souls caused by a profit-making capitalist system. But these progressive reformers were to be disappointed by the end of the Second World War. New Dealers had hoped to develop "yardstick" industries which would challenge capitalism. Oskar Lange, the socialist planner, had described how the government could set up its own enterprises, challenging capitalism to do better. The TVA was the first and last major attempt at such an enterprise.

The attitude of liberals with regard to corporations was one of ambivalence. Henry Wallace, for example, both applauded and berated the corporations. He feared that if "the rate which the 200 largest corporations have been growing since 1909 is maintained in the future they will control 70 per cent of our corporate wealth by 1950." * [12] Yet, he felt that capitalism could be tamed. He believed that there was a class of capitalists who, because of their pragmatic orientation, would be progressive. For him this meant that they would favor the opening of more markets through trade, aggressive sales, and well-run assembly lines.[13]

Whether they were "good" corporations or "bad" corporations, the reality was that the executive government acted as the facilitator for the largest business enterprises.[14] Through the President, business-dominated government committees were organized which protected the growth of big business and assumed that the growth of the largest corporations was the primary way to develop American civilization. It has been a cardinal principle that big business helps big government and vice versa. This arrangement has been called a "Partnership" by Presidents Eisenhower, Kennedy, Johnson, and Nixon. During this entire

---

* The corporation's steady growth has turned out to be remarkably on schedule. By 1960, the 500 largest corporations accounted for 70 percent of profits and 60 percent of sales, although they represented only one-fourth of 1 percent of the number of industries in the country.

period, Congress remained local, sectional, and cranky. But its orneriness did not stop Congress from capitulating to the big-government/big-business partnership, while heaping privileges and power onto the Executive for "management" and "emergency" purposes. It has been a cardinal principle of American government that the government was to have "every power requisite to the full accomplishment of the objective committed to its care." [15] By the time of the second Roosevelt, however, this principle had come to mean that government was to be synonymous with presidential power.

For example, in 1933 a frightened Congress, in the midst of national crisis, turned to the Executive. They expected the President to formulate his program and to "act." It was generally accepted that the ideas which the members of Congress had about the economic depression did not seem to speak to the changed realities. They added up to a cacophony of voices out of tune with the times. According to the *New York Times* columnist Anne O'Hare McCormick, a distinguished senator had said:

> Why should we be the scapegoat? If we had rejected some inspired plans for national recovery, any plan, in fact, we might reasonably be damned. But not a single group in the country, businessmen, industrialists, bankers, labor leaders, not a single individual, from the President down, has yet to come before us with a real program or constructive suggestion. No, the country pretends it expects nothing of Congress and now condemns us for doing what nobody can do. We are blamed if we act and if we don't act. Having led us to ruin, the great business brains in the country can think of nothing but to berate this contemptible body for not pulling them out. [16]

The President, of course, did not have any better idea of what to do. His own staffs were split during the depression on the development of a coherent policy—except that of action qua action.* Roosevelt encouraged and expected Congress to pass laws that were general delegations of power. The President and his advisers could figure out what to do *after* they had the power and authority to act. It has been taken for granted since Roosevelt II that this is the Age of Crisis which requires greater power to be exercised by fewer people. Rarely has it been considered that the Age of Crisis might have been caused by this principle of governing.

Since 1933, the United States has been in a declared state of national emergency and crisis. During this period Congress delegated, through 580 code sections, discretionary authority to the President "which taken all together, confer the power to rule this country without reference to normal constitutional processes." [17] Indeed, as one Senate Committee report pointed out, "No charge can be sustained that the Executive branch has usurped powers belonging to the Legislative branch." [18] Under the powers delegated by these statutes, the President may seize properties, mobilize production, seize commodities, institute martial law, seize control of all transportation and communications, regulate private capital, restrict travel, and—in a host of particular and peculiar ways—control the activities of all American citizens. Of course, all this power was legislatively granted to the President. It did not represent individual initiatives and residual power which the President could claim for himself under Article II of the Constitution. It is now assumed that a President may act in the national interest in any way he sees fit, "provided he was not prohibited by the Constitution from doing it" [Steel-seizure case].[19] In other words, it is the Executive who is to fill all the spaces of the society (and the world!) with his will and action, so long as he is not specifically proscribed from acting.

---

* They did agree, finally, to sustain the largest possible units of social organization through such mechanisms as the National Recovery Administration (NRA).

American constitutional law provides ample support for the principle that if a President warrants his actions on the political grounds of necessity and the principle of inherent powers, he retains the authority to refuse to spend funds or to enforce laws. If his counselors do not care to rely on the emergency laws passed by Congress—which the Supreme Court ruled in the *Youngstown* case were valid—a President may look to his implied or inherent power.[20] A President can refer to *Mississippi v. Johnson*, in which the Supreme Court held that it could not enjoin a President from exceeding his powers or refusing to perform his constitutional duties.[21] The Court held in that case, and in *Marbury v. Madison*, that a President was accountable only to his conscience.* [22]

Leaving aside the actions of Abraham Lincoln during the Civil War, presidential supremacy found its boldest statement on September 7, 1942. In the midst of the Second World War, the President said of the Emergency Price Control Act that unless the Congress acted in the way he wanted, he would accept the responsibility and act himself. The President was saying that the Executive could collapse the legislative authority into his own authority. As Professor Edward Corwin, a leading constitutional scholar, pointed out, President Roosevelt was claiming for himself "the power and the right to disregard a statutory provision that he did not challenge, and indeed could not possibly have

* In case some members of the modern Supreme Court feel otherwise, a President can deal with them in other ways. Richard Nixon undertook to intimidate members of the Supreme Court through Attorney General John Mitchell. Together, they were able to force Abe Fortas, a civil libertarian with many connections to corporations, from the Supreme Court, ostensibly because of his involvement with Louis Wolfson. They thereby served notice on other judges that they were not invulnerable or insulated—especially since updated files and reports were kept on the judges by the Justice Department. Swollen with the political corpse of the insecure and soiled Fortas, Mitchell and Nixon then attempted, unsuccessfully, to remove William O. Douglas. With Gerald Ford as their manager, they generated over one hundred motions of impeachment in the House against Douglas. Besides Nixon's own efforts at intimidation, fortune now seemed to smile on him. He was able to name four justices to the Supreme Court who, he

challenged." 2 3 He could make his own higher law, based on his view of necessity, and on the political rule that the President is the highest authority. Thus, when Congress did not pass emergency legislation, Roosevelt taught Congress and future Presidents that a President was bound only by what Rex Tugwell called "the rule of necessity."

It is not surprising that Roosevelt's assertion (or the extraordinary powers claimed by Lincoln and Wilson before him) came during wartime. The second major justification for executive prerogative, after that of economic stability and growth, is the President's claim to be the guardian of national security. Since 1933, Congress has given the President virtually total discretion on matters of national security—a slippery phrase which the President can define any way that pleases him so that it can encompass both foreign and domestic policy. The blandishments and reasons of interest groups, whether the Associated Milk Producers or the aerospace industrialists, could be held secret behind the mask of executive privilege—another claim of executive right which Nixon hoped to make absolute. Since 1940, the national security argument has been used widely to hide mean or dastardly acts of government officials and their friends. These acts related either to the nature of war and imperialism or to the spread of the capitalist ethic to government and administration. Why was it important to hide these actions? For a generation, American Presidents were pulled more and more deeply into the world of violence and illegality through the military and spying

---

believed, would favor his arguments about a strong Executive and who would be especially supportive of activities which his government would seek to justify on grounds of national security. (However, by a vote of 8-0, even Nixon's loosely packed Supreme Court rejected the unlimited right of wiretap on grounds of national security [407 U.S. 297 (1972)].) As to the lower courts, Nixon intended to "appoint judges who will help to strengthen the peace forces as against the criminal forces in the country" [November 4, 1972]. Thus, Nixon made it clear that he and his retinue viewed the courts as well as the Congress as window dressing to cover the actual processes of the modern authoritarian state.

system that propped up imperialism. By the time of Nixon's Presidency, a President's day was spent in activities that were more criminal than political, from plotting wars to buying foreign government officials.

Up until the revelation concerning the break-in of Daniel Ellsberg's psychiatrist's office, the Congress, the courts, and the American people had been told that the President and members of the executive branch were to define national security unilaterally, generally on the basis of secret information which they refused to share with the people, the other branches of government, other parts of the bureaucracy, or indeed, within their own bureaucracy. The President, acting daily as commander-in-chief of the armed forces and of the federal paramilitary forces, such as the Central Intelligence Agency (CIA),* claimed justification for the exercise of executive powers on grounds of *emergency and national security which are personally or subjectively defined by the man who happens to be President.*

The phrase "national security" conjures up in the American mind decisions and actions based on the highest motives and intentions. Yet an analysis of the decisions taken by Presidents and their national security managers, as Richard Barnet has pointed out, will show the tawdriness of those decisions and of the men who made them.[24] Whether it was the Cuban missile crisis which grew out of President Kennedy's wish to stop the sniping of Senator Kenneth Keating of New York and make a strong Democratic party showing in the 1962 Congressional elections; whether it was the buying up of the French and Italian labor unions to ensure the victory of Christian Democratic forces during the Truman and Eisenhower periods; whether it was the funding of coups in Nicaragua and Guatemala, or the continuous squander-

---

* Senator Stuart Symington has referred to the CIA as the President's army.

ing of funds on militarism—the motive for these actions can be interpreted only as a calculated evasion of the American domestic situation, an evasion Americans have embraced.

Overwhelmed by economic insecurity and a sense of personal powerlessness, bedeviled by an inadequate social security, welfare, and work system and by the massive ripping up of cities and employment migrations, Americans have been offered national security as the ideological substitute for reform and reconstruction at home. The national security mentality in the government, on Wall Street, La Salle Street, and the Pentagon, has helped to rationalize the American empire and the symbiotic relationship between imperialism and the business, bureaucratic, scientific, military, and internal security elites. These elites used the presidential Office and the immense taxing authority of the United States to support imperial forces around the world, protect special taxing advantages to corporations, and turn every attempted social reform into a cardboard or pornographic copy of the real coin.

Practically speaking, such executive principles of governing can be secured only by funds, military power, ideology, and an active bureaucracy. Since the New Deal—especially in national security affairs—extraordinary sums of money have been made available through congressional appropriations to the President, a process that requires the cooptation of congressional leadership. Such cooptation is accomplished through discussion, personal favors, and privileges granted by the White House, the military, and the bureaucracy to individual congressional leaders. The congressional committee system, which allows chairmen to act for the committee as a whole, is easily coopted into the executive net. As a general rule, congressional chairmen see themselves as the permanent undersecretaries of the bureaucracy. Scarcity of means, which once operated to limit a ruler who tended to absolutism, has long since disappeared. On his own initiative, with "proper advice" from ruling elites, a President can make war on his own, commit troops, and develop "national security needs" which require vast resources in people and materials. Such requirements may be dressed up in the complex language of the nuclear strategist, but the "needs" and "appetites" of Presidents are little different from those of the European kings who hunted recruits on village streets and feudal farms while taxing for purposes of personal glory and the maintenance of lavish palace courts. In our time, a President is able to whittle and change programs, transfer and hide funds so that Congress is transformed into another audience which may withhold its applause but not affect the course of the play.

The development of the national security mentality and the national security state, combined with the notion of the President acting in the general welfare, provided the administrative, economic, and political foundation upon which the empire was built. It strengthened the nonsocial welfare aspects of state power and secured the profitable expansion of capitalism. Traditional distinctions between war and peace, between permanent engagement and intervention, were no longer made. The state was engaged and the President operated through the screen of the bureaucracy, with advice pulled from spies, robber barons, or their representatives and generals. This was the way man's fate was to be decided. Thus, if a John Kennedy perceived a threat to American interests in Laos or Cuba, the "protection of national security" allowed him to call upon his power as commander-in-chief to direct the military, the economy, and the American psyche along a particular path. National security added fuel to the principle that the President has indefinite powers which allowed him to justify any direction in which he cared to take the country. When John Ehrlichman stated as much to the Senate Watergate

Committee, his language came as a very great surprise to the media and the American public.[25] However, his stated views were not that different from those set forth by Lincoln and all modern American Presidents. The difference was that the modern principle of benevolent dictatorship had been moved by Nixon and his clique to a rawer stage.

2 Nixon Before the Storm: Supreme Survivor and Master Politician

One of the ironies of politics is that through March 1973, Nixon had near-universal support as a survivor and master politician. Against all political wisdom, he had survived the defeats and embarrassments of the 1960s to win nomination and election in 1968. He had done so despite fervent political opposition based on a well-founded distrust of the man and his methods. He was hailed as a master politician. Not only was he able to "package" himself for public consumption, but Nixon also allowed his retinue to package him in any way they saw fit so that he would be salable to diverse groups.

Yet Nixon was a known political quantity. He was a "law and order" man of the pragmatic right who believed in Authority. He was insecure and aloof personally, despising weakness and admiring winners. He did not hesitate to make sharp turns with policy, programs and people, knowing from his past and his experience in imperial politics that "rectitude, self sacrifice, good faith have never been anywhere or at any time the qualities that best serve for attaining power and holding it." [1] Nevertheless, he believed that it was necessary to cultivate appearances. "Men in general," Machiavelli had said, "are as much affected by what things seem to be as by what they are; often indeed, they are moved more by the appearances than by the reality of things." [2] Nixon had publicly identified himself as a believer in lying. During the 1960 campaign, Nixon was trapped into appearing to be "softer" on Castro than was President Kennedy. He was forced to pretend to be against the Bay of Pigs invasion of Cuba, and in favor of American treaty obligations not to invade Cuba. In retrospect, he said,

> I was sure then, and I am sure now, that the position I had to take on Cuba hurt rather than helped me. The average voter is not interested in the technicalities of treaty obligations. He thinks, quite properly, that Castro is a menace, and he favors the candidate who wants to do something about it—something positive and dramatic and forceful—and not the one who takes the "statesmanlike" and the "legalistic" view.[3]

Nixon as President, then, developed a series of appearances. He affected a style of distance and technical skill, feigned concern with grand conceptions, and pretended little interest in the details (the plays) or the instruments of government. He wanted to develop a style of government that would appear contemplative and thorough. He criticized, therefore, the bustle of the life of the street and the bureaucracy alike. He believed that "getting away from the White House, from the Oval office, from that 100 yards that one walks every day from the President's bedroom to the President's office or the extra 50 yards across to the EOB, getting away gives a sense of perspective. . . . I find that up here on top of the mountain [Camp David] it is easier for me to get on top of the job." [4] Like a character from a "beat" novel of the 1950s, Nixon found that he was rootless and without place. There was no place where he felt comfortable, where he would not be "interrupted either physically or personally or in any other way." [5] His restlessness manifested itself in his many trips to recently acquired homes at the ends of America. Like so many Americans, he felt himself an émigré in his own country. His closest adviser, the refugee Henry Kissinger, was the embodiment of this émigré status.

Nixon was also a romantic. He believed in the cult of the ordinary and in the success that could come to ordinary white men through the American System. His friends, Robert Abplanalp and Clement Stone and Bebe Rebozo, were proof that ambition, competition, and packaging the hard work of others were absolute values that the God of Billy Graham and Cardinal Spellman rewarded and justified through the American System. Like Lyndon Johnson, he believed in "a country in which a man or a woman has an equal chance at that starting line and an equal chance to go to the top." Nixon stood with Woodrow Wilson in believing that the battlers and the scufflers from the middle level of American life were its backbone, and with his election they had come into their own—and into power.

Nixon modeled himself after de Gaulle's public image. De Gaulle was inaccessible. He took the long view. He was conservative and had come to power on the backs of the Right and the colonels. Yet he knew full well that he would have to liquidate the Algerian war and turn against his rightist constituency. De Gaulle believed in grandeur. On Nixon, such ideas fit like someone else's clothes. Where de Gaulle seemed to speak for glory, tradition and the great enterprise, Nixon seemed to have no tradition beyond that of winning games, being "tough" and the homily to "keep trying." He was plagued with a neurotic quality of suppressed

Quakerism; he was hostile, paranoid, angry, and self-pitying. Yet, hidden behind clichés, he had a powerful and warped intellect, and a formidable capacity to "stay" when others wanted him "out." Eisenhower had tried, first in 1952 and then in 1956, to get Nixon off his ticket. But to no avail. Eisenhower used public ridicule, but he capitulated to Nixon's flypaper qualities. Where de Gaulle's style created a political consciousness, however fetid, Nixon could operate only through his clique against parliamentary institutions—using advertising slogans as his rhetoric. Both showed their obvious contempt for representative institutions upon whom the appearance of deference must be showered. And both suffered for their contempt.

Nixon's mode of ruling was by coopting issues, but not people. His staff would read the newspapers carefully, and in daily digest form Nixon learned from them what was going on in the society. His task, as he saw it, was to inoculate the groups on the streets, in the board rooms, or in the Congress by stating that he and his administration were aware of the problem and by promising that his aides would deal with it. Nixon's mode differed from that of the Democratic party which coopted leaders of movements or interests ("problems") into a party and ruling system. By 1972 there were Democrats saying that men could not represent women, rich people could not represent poor people, and whites could not represent nonwhites. Nixon played on this point of view and used its fervor, adding talk about states' rights and the New Federalism. Nixon, attracted to the police and repressive powers of the state, covered a profoundly authoritarian direction with the rhetoric of returning power to the people.

In spite of the narrow margin of victory in 1968, Nixon's aides had every reason to believe that Nixon was totally supported by the people. After a decade of turbulence, Nixon and his group judged that the people were bored with the political and congressional process. Nixon thought that concern for free speech, assembly, and public discussion in the legislative bodies was restricted to a very few. The people, in his view, craved mainly to be let alone and to leave government to a master—Nixon. Seeking solace in heavily guarded sanctuaries, from the mountains of Appalachia to the oceans of the Atlantic and Pacific, he thought that the best decisions could be made in private and that the "mob" in Congress and on the streets affirmed his need to act privately and secretively.

Nixon agreed with his first vice-president that this mob had no rights. He believed that a President was elected by the people as a ruler. An American President could do pretty much as he wanted. In a speech emphasizing the return of power to the people (by which he really meant government by plebiscite), he made clear his own views about the Presidency:

> In the years to come, if I am returned to office, I shall not hesitate to take the action I think necessary to protect and defend this Nation's best interests, whether or not those actions meet with wide popular approval.[6]

As we have seen, such views had an impressive pedigree; Nixon was the beneficiary of a liberal legacy of presidential supremacy and authority that had been trumpeted since Theodore Roosevelt by scholars and commentators alike. For over sixty years, people had been told incessantly that the President alone was the embodiment of the National Will, its interests and aspirations. Nixon himself believed this presidential principle. He knew also of congressional willingness to give massive power to a President, having watched Senator Robert Taft reviled by his own colleagues for attempting to salvage some vestige of congressional power in the face of strong bureaucracy. From this perspective, Nixon spent his first term defining his political direction and sculpting a government to match his purpose.

Nixon and Agnew came to power in 1969, having ridden the crest of disenchantment with the war in Indochina and the defection of part of the working and middle classes from the Democratic party. They believed that they could play upon the eruptions of the universities and the turmoil in the streets to their advantage, thus identifying and exploiting the distaste which George Wallace's supporters and workers felt toward the massive stylistic and cultural changes of the 1960s. Yet Nixon and Agnew also feared the demonstrators, their new life styles, and their disrespect for Authority. The two men therefore favored Draconian measures which reflected the substance of martial law without directly suspending the courts and the public bodies. This way they hoped to form and win the allegiance of a right-wing working class: a volatile group that might organize offensively with George Wallace to obtain the Presidency.

Agnew believed that the demonstrations and disruptions of the privileged on the streets and in the universities would strengthen such "uncontrollable" forces and bring internal repression beyond what even the administration said it wanted. At the time the Huston Memorandum was secretly debated by the FBI, the CIA, White House Defense Intelligence Agency, and the National Security Agency, Agnew told audiences that it was necessary to set up strong authoritarian measures "before the witch hunting and repression that are all too inevitable begin." [7] Authoritarianism was necessary to stop "vigilante" activities. Agnew wanted to "separate the rotten apples" so that totalitarianism, as he put it, could be prevented. To do this required "firm, decisive action and a willingness to withstand the criticism of the liberal community who are presently so blinded by total dedication to individual freedom." [8] The liberals, Nixon and Agnew believed, allowed the counterculture to flourish, vitiating the old authoritarian and paternalistic values. The result was a weakened American resolve.

In domestic policy, Nixon broke the antipoverty program, the Democratic party's attempt at social welfare and control over the poor. He preferred the development of a strengthened internal police and surveillance system which would eliminate the politically threatening possibility that middle-income government workers, like social workers and storefront lawyers, might make common cause with their clients against the newly emerging authoritarian system. And, by the end of his first term, Democratic political leaders lined up to agree that the antipoverty program "didn't work." Instead, there was an emerging consensus around Vice-President Agnew's position toward the militarization of the polity. The "cop on the beat . . . is on our side in the war against crime. His uniform is the uniform of our troops. A policeman's badge should command the same respect granted a soldier's green beret, a sailor's dolphin." [9]

Agnew and Nixon's brand of authority found its responsive chord among those who believed in the centrality of paternalism and untrammeled capitalism. Nixon, who had preached to Chicano children that they should respect their parents and the church, told the Texas ruling class that the poor people were not interested in the "call for redistribution of income, to see that those who do not work are rewarded more than those who do. When those children wanted to come to Washington they didn't ask those rich oil men [to] put up the money," he said.[10] They did it according to Nixon's view of the American way. They earned the money themselves by washing cars, baby sitting, and selling "those good Texas tamales for fifty cents. . . . They didn't want something for nothing, and that is the kind of spirit we need in America." [11] Nixon had ordered the impoundment of funds and the violation of congressional intent, to ensure that the working class and the poor did not get "something for nothing."

It was in foreign policy that the public adoration for Nixon's "technical skill" was most frequently expressed. Lost wars bring to power new cliques and a scrambling for institutional and social redefinition. Except for Henry Kissinger, Nixon and his group of processors were, in the main, different from those who ran the national security state from the time of Colonel Henry Stimson, the Wall Street patrician who was chosen to be the secretary of war in 1940 over Mayor La Guardia who represented an urban populist sentiment.

The direction of national security had been in the hands of a very narrow elite for an entire generation. Nixon had watched its development and was not unmindful of its successes. He had long favored their imperial goals. He believed in intervention and protectorate status for Southeast Asia and the "entire free world." Nixon believed in the objectives of American policy makers who entered the Second World War in defense of a newly acquired sphere of influence over Southeast Asia. He had suggested in 1954 that nuclear weapons should be used at Dien Bien Phu.[12] During the same period, Henry Kissinger, then adviser to the Rockefeller family, had endeavored to work out rules for the use of nuclear weapons.[13] But Nixon doubted the abilities of the eastern elites to maintain control of the empire. He thought they no longer knew what was in their interests or, indeed, how to protect them. Many of the southern senators concurred in this view.

The authoritarian senators, like John Stennis (Mississippi) and Richard Russell (Georgia), believed that the war in Indochina turned out to be an institutional disaster for the American military hierarchy. The military was forced to make peace by its own soldiers, who gave up fighting in the field. Even some of the dependable ones, the American airmen, showed a changed attitude about their own warmaking role with various members of the air force courting mutiny charges because they were unwilling to load bombs. The foot soldiers deserted or shot into the air. Such were the daily reports sent to the joint chiefs of staff by CINCPAC in 1971 and 1972. The chiefs were aware that "we have reduced our total military manpower by nearly one third from the 1968 level." [14] And they knew it was not out of any theory of arms control or forward planning, but because Congress no longer cared to support militarist privileges for unsuccessful adventures.* While the Democrats under Kennedy had decreed that the United States should be able to fight two and a half wars simultaneously, the military chiefs now had to contend with the Nixon-Kissinger foreign policy which appeared to—but did not—call for cutbacks in military force to the so-called one-and-a-half-war theory and greater reliance on proxy forces. Nixon put the new defense policy in the following way:

> The stated basis of our conventional posture in the 1960's was the so-called "2 and one half war" principle. According to it, U.S. forces would be maintained for a three month conventional forward defense of NATO, a defense of Korea or Southeast Asia against a full scale Chinese attack, and a minor contingency—all simultaneously. These force levels were never reached.
>
> In the effort to harmonize doctrine and capability, we chose what is best described as the 1 and one half war strategy. Under it we will maintain in peacetime general purpose forces adequate to simultaneously meeting a major Communist attack in either Europe or Asia, assisting allies against non Chinese threats in Asia, and contending with contingency elsewhere. [15]

Nixon's foreign policy created the impression that American military imperialism would take a back seat to more traditional practices of foreign policy. The political ghost of Chester Bowles (the undersecretary of state sacked by President Kennedy for his liberal and mildly anti-imperialist views) seemed to speak

---

* In 1974 the secretary of defense attempted to increase the military's privilege and power by asserting that it was necessary to achieve a healthy economy.

through Nixon's first secretary of state. "The Nixon Doctrine," said Secretary William Rogers, "represents a recognition that protection of our national interest does not require an automatic U.S. military response to every threat."[16] Once the direct American military engagement seemed to have ended in Indochina, Nixon reverted to the imperialist principle of rule by indirection, expending $2.5 billion yearly on the client state of South Vietnam—an amount equal to federal expenditures on internal police forces within the United States, exclusive of state expenditure on internal military forces. Congressional liberals came to believe that in foreign policy Nixon was doing their bidding.

Having built his career on anticommunism, whether of the Russian or the Chinese kind, Nixon expected and received adulation from the liberals for having "ended" the cold war with both. Of course, it was he as much as any other single figure of the post-World War II generation who created an atmosphere against détente, who led in the hunting down of dentists, government officials, liberals, academics, anyone who suggested that there should be a détente with the Russians and Chinese. Then, in jiujitsu fashion, he confiscated the platform of those liberals who had favored a détente and trade with China and the Soviet Union. Nixon's brazenness and the short memories of Americans will be a source of wonder for future generations. As President, he received the applause of the liberals whom he had frustrated for twenty-five years. Early in 1973, Senator Edward Kennedy, at a dinner honoring a conservative Democratic fund raiser, chose to applaud the President for his foreign policies and foresight.

The paradox for Nixon was that the Republican party was nowhere near supporting his wide-ranging diplomatic initiatives. Nor, for that matter, was the national security bureaucracy. Nixon found himself developing his own organization, designed to circumvent the bureaucracy in some cases and rebuff the Republican party by developing a system of alliances and allegiances directly between himself and particular corporations and interest groups.

In his first term, Nixon surrounded himself with men who reflected his own values and beliefs—Magruder, Dean, Ehrlichman, Haldeman, Mitchell, Colson, Chapin, Hunt, Segretti, Kalmbach, Liddy, Gray, LaRue, and Krogh. Traditional bureaucrats from the CIA called this group *The Outfit*. Nixon's men were organizational processors drawn from the CIA, FBI, armed forces, suburban law partnerships, and huge advertising firms. Either by experience, as in the case of the senior processors, or by demonstrated inclination in the case of their apprentices, the processors showed an instinctive understanding of and commitment to the values and policies of the battlers and scufflers. The processor mind applauds efficiency and accomplishment of task—whatever it is. The "whys" and "wherefores" are not to be asked. Because the *processor* sees relationships through the prism of hierarchy and authority, he assumes that the moral questions are already resolved. As Jeb Magruder, deputy chairman of CREEP, told those who worked for Nixon: "You've got to do what the hierarchy wants, that's why you're here. In the corporate life you must conform or it can be very difficult." [17] "These are men," Nixon once said, that "money can't buy." They were responsible to a leader and owed their allegiance and new-found fame and fortune to Nixon.

For Nixon, these men were the symbols of the updated Babbitry in American life which he saw as the pride of the nation itself. They were the excellent average. As some of the liberal columnists sanctimoniously chorused, the middle American could now believe that "his kind" was in charge. The political problem for such men, when they come to power, is that they have no roots and are easily used or isolated by those with rooted power. Most of Nixon's men did not come out of the matured baronies of American society and were not the political representatives of those baronies—whether the labor unions, great corporations, or the universities. As a result, they were men easily stripped of governmental power and authority because they were unable to call on vast economic, political, and social groups within the society to rally to their defense or support their positions. It is not surprising, then, that the list prepared late in his first term by Nixon's staff of his political enemies reflected *all* elements of American life which had a measure of national power that was independent or rooted. The list was made up of diverse characters: Governor Wallace of the right wing; Thomas Watson, the IBM corporate interest magnate; and Bobby Seale of the street Left. (Even this author.)

Nixon had believed that his men were virtuosos in the sense that Machiavelli had thought of virtuosos of politics and power—namely, unexcelled ability to accomplish successfully ends defined by the leader, the Prince. In the modern period, the passive audience—the public—is supposed to ratify the "good works" of the leader and his *virtuosi* through elections and public-opinion polls. The methods the leader might use to secure his good works—whether threats, bribes, atomic bombs, magic, or "sweeteners"—are unimportant. He can adopt any of these and expect the processor to translate the decision into action and the audience to applaud uncritically.

But most leaders are as confused as the processors. Leaders have no more idea of what is to be done or how than the processor does. Moreover, the leader often confuses loyalty with political skill and virtue, thus relying heavily on those who appear to be the most obedient. The audience and the media may designate a processor as a man of power in his own right. And the processor, emboldened by this new view of himself and his own demystified

view of leadership, invokes the name of the leader for his purposes which—if they are in a generally accepted framework—the
leader will adopt, and adopt as his own. (In this sense Henry
Kissinger was a successful processor who became a leader.
Others, like Ehrlichman, were not so successful.) Nixon, as we
have seen, had only the vaguest sense of program. But he did have
a central purpose. President Nixon by his second term seemed to
want to move out of the position of being a broker of a national
and "social" security *System* which had been fashioned since the
New Deal. To achieve his purpose of developing a new leadership
principle, each of the processors had been assigned very specific
tasks during Nixon's first term. These tasks were calculated to
liberate the President, in his second term, from dependency on
either the Republican party, the recalcitrants in the bureaucracy
and Congress, or the citizenry. The tasks manifest the Nixon
principles of how things work:

> The congressional Republican party was downgraded and
> shunned. (Ehrlichman and Haldeman)
> The Democrats were cast as enemies of the state and sover-
> eign. They were surveilled, confronted, and, if necessary,
> personally discredited. (Colson, Chapin, and Haldeman)
> Phones were tapped with an increase in break-ins, burg-
> laries, entrapment. (Mitchell, Mardian, and Ehrlichman)
> A series of working groups under a Cabinet Committee to
> Combat Terrorism was set up to "insure governmentwide
> cooperation in the sharing" of information and plans.
> Political dissidents were controlled through limited martial
> law, informers, harassment, and entrapment. (Rehnquist,
> Mardian, Kleindienst, and Mitchell)

Universities and schools were encouraged to adopt stringent rules of behavior and admissions standards expelling students who did not comply. Grants and federal contracts were withheld from unfriendly university administrations. (Agnew and Colson)

National security became a justification to eliminate any type of politics deemed threatening. (Mitchell and Kissinger)

Members of the bureaucracy were watched and bugged for any signs of disloyalty. (Haldeman, Ehrlichman, Mitchell, and Kissinger)

Secret wars were fought and secret negotiations were carried on without the knowledge of the Congress and without any form of accountability. (Kissinger, Laird, and the Joint Chiefs of Staff)

Police budgets were substantially increased with federal funds used for equipment, centralization and quasi-militarization of the police. (Kleindienst and Santarelli)

Millions of dollars collected through CREEP were controlled by Nixon's personal lawyer. The funds were used for any purpose the President and his clique deemed necessary. (Kalmbach and Ehrlichman)

A "metic" class was to be authorized through "social welfare" legislation. (Ehrlichman)

When and where necessary, such activities were hidden with the claim of executive privilege. (Kleindienst and Dean)

There was an attempt to develop a domestic council which would "encourage closer cooperation between the various federal agencies and their state and local counterparts" taken at the "recommendation" of Agnew and Colson and Ehrlichman.

The media was intimidated. (Agnew, Buchanan, and White-head)

Under the guise of saving money, congressionally appropriated funds were not spent except for projects which the President had cleared. In other words, the President would set and enforce his own social priorities in the face of laws and acts of Congress. (Weinberger, Shultz, Malek, and Ash)

Nixon's processors were not without enemies on the Right. They were thought of as unprincipled by the Goldwater wing. Virtually all Republican congressmen complained of high-handed or indifferent treatment by the White House. They were accused, in the Washington parlance, of knowing the price of everything, but the value of nothing. Men like Senators Goldwater and Strom Thurmond, reserve generals, did not believe in Nixon's policy of détente with the Chinese and Russians. They represented the military point of view, and the military leadership was decidedly unhappy with its own slipping place in the American political pantheon. Harsh critiques of the military, formerly reserved to leftist journals like the *Progressive*, *The Nation*, and *Liberation*, found their way into the *New York Times*, budgetary debates in Congress, and even GI newspapers.

However, Nixon grew in confidence as he survived year-by-year in office. He began his campaign for a second term, saying that he knew how he intended to govern for "four more years." He believed himself to be a supreme survivor and master politician. "We know how things work here," he said. "Ehrlichman's crowd, Kissinger's crowd, they know how things work. . . . We don't want too violent a change. We know all the plays. We're going to be in a position to present to the country changes in the system that will work."[18] John Mitchell, Nixon's very close friend, gleefully announced prior to the second term that the administration was going to move so far to the right that the country would be unrecognizable in a few years. Mitchell and Maurice Stans intended to accomplish this feat with corporate acquiescence and collaboration. A word needs to be said about the business imperative which Nixon and his group so admired.

In *The Accumulation of Capital*, Rosa Luxemburg discusses the need of capital to find new markets. "It is quite irrelevant to the present field of accumulation, when where and how the capital of the old countries has been realized so that it may flow into the new country. British *capital which finds an outlet in Argentine railway construction might well in the past have been realized in China in the form of Indian opium.*" [19] The search for higher profits will invariably include expansion into foreign countries where state structures are weak and therefore legal structures are very favorable to new capital.

Luxemburg's example is striking for our purposes because it goes to the issue of crime (opium). Capital will seek markets where it can find markets of profit. In the previous several generations, the ideology of the corporation and of silk-stocking reformers has revolved around the question of how government and corporations could work together to keep mobsters out of the mature corporations and the operations of finance and investment capital. The issue, as brought out in Watergate, seems to be the reverse. What we see instead is the number of large enterprises who will undertake to invest their earnings in criminal activity. Two parallel directions are discerned for the American corporation. One is its escape abroad to find markets and investment opportunities, so that ultimately it has no home, merely transactions and operations. The other is through investment in crime —for example, gambling and drugs. In criminal activity, there are larger bonuses because the operations are based on the most central principles of capitalism—the ability and the will to buy and sell *anything*. Even certain legitimate businessmen will dip into criminal activity when it becomes necessary to secure markets.

During the Senate hearings on multinational corporations, it was revealed that ITT offered a million dollars to U.S. government officials to spend the way they thought best in order to stop Allende from coming to power.[20] As in Chicago and Philadelphia, so also in Venezuela, American voting-machine manufacturers bribed government officials so that "free elections" could be held with the latest equipment. Bribery is an important instrument for businessmen when they want to break into a new market but find that the laws restrict entry of newcomers. (Thus the SEC and Robert Vesco.) Regulatory commissions are the governmental shield for the protection of "mature" corporations. The bribe system is generally unnecessary for "mature" corporations which can dictate or shape the laws and regulations guiding their respective industry.*[21]

Island economies like the Bahamas become an "inevitable" place for gamblers and crooks who come together with legitimate financiers and bankers. The President's friend Bebe Rebozo opened his bank to investment opportunities of this sort.[22] The Nixon group found itself involved in a series of criminal activities that were initiated by businessmen as well as by themselves. Although Nixon's processors extorted funds from corporations for his campaign, many businessmen still saw themselves as protected in their activities by Nixon. Furthermore, they found it useful to help him, a relatively poor man, as things go in American politics. The businessman on the make, the country club set

---

* Thus, when George Humphrey became the secretary of the treasury under President Eisenhower, one of his first acts was to arrange a fast tax write-off which netted an immediate saving of $100 million for two of his companies "with the immediate private gain to Secretary Humphrey greater than the entire treasuries of most unions in the country." Neither firm had to bribe anyone to get the regulations changed.

tinged with crime, was Nixon's natural constituency. While he courted little businessmen and big businessmen, assuring them markets wherever they could find them, by his second term Nixon had terminated any such pattern of favors or privileges or courtesies with respect to Congress.

Traditionally, in order to coopt Congress, Presidents in the past spent time in fraudulent consultations, politically "stroking" congressional officials. Such stroking gave members of Congress the illusion of participating in decision making. It allowed them the fantasy that they were powerful as well as privileged. Presidential stroking had a more immediate payoff for the congressional member as well. He would retail such sessions with a President to his constituency, thereby securing his own position by showing his importance. Nixon breached this etiquette and failed to pay obeisance to constitutional form. He and his clique did not want to be bothered, and in any case, Nixon had told them they needed only one-third of either House in order for him to do what he wanted with the country. This perception allowed Nixon to be free of caring about the political fortunes of congressional candidates.

To prove his independence and authority, Nixon chose a path separate from the Republican party in 1972. He did not actively campaign for other Republican candidates. In one sense, the American political system implicitly endorsed and condoned such behavior. A presidential aspirant, especially an incumbent, is supposed to be beyond politics. He is presented to the public as representing all interests. "Politics" had meant that quality within a person which is self-serving, ambitious, and quite contemptible. According to Nixon's Secretary of Defense James Schlesinger, politics is "the art of calculated cheating." [23] Indeed, people (even political parties) campaign for public office on the claim of being nonpolitical. This is due to an assumption, deeply embedded in the tradition of the Founding Fathers and thus in American politics, that it is the

> propensity of mankind to fall into mutual animosities, that where no substantial occasion presents itself the most frivolous and fanciful distinctions have been sufficient to kindle their unfriendly passions and excite their most violent conflicts. . . . Men of facetious tempers, of local prejudices, or of sinister designs may, by intrigue, by corruption, or by other means, first obtain the suffrage, and then betray the interests of the people.[24]

In 1972, Nixon manifested very little interest in his political party as the instrument for organizing the different forces in American life, nor was he overly concerned with the fortunes of Republican officeholders. He rationalized his separation from party on the "coattails" principle: if he won reelection, the Republicans would "benefit" in any case. Even if Nixon's rationalization had political merit, he seemed to have overlooked another purpose of the political party: It is a cementing system which brings together local bourgeois interests with national and international interests. It ties the several million petty officials, elected through the party structure, to the President. The political party is the means by which political power outside the ongoing state bureaucratic apparatus is communicated and exchanged among *all* American government officials. Such interaction is especially crucial where a President believes that constitutional forms are mere window dressing and that legitimation is an accidental act. Nixon believed, for example, that the 1960 presidential election had been stolen from him by Richard Daley's Democratic party in Illinois. Yet he did not have the modern totalitarian's instinctive understanding that a strong party apparatus can successfully replace constitutional forms. The party, not the election, becomes the method of guiding the direction of the people—or of keeping in touch with them.

It should be said in President Nixon's defense, however, that he believed the elective process could be manipulated *from* the White House for the benefit of himself and his party. After all, in the twentieth century, only William Taft and Herbert Hoover lost reelection as incumbents. Nixon did not operate the Presidency from their set of scruples, nor did he have their political problems. Because Hoover and Taft saw presidential power as being in conflict with capitalism and "private" property, these men believed that there were limits to the power of the presidential office and, therefore, of the federal establishment as a whole. Indeed, President Taft had said that the "President can exercise no power which cannot be fairly and reasonably traced to some specific grant of power or justly implied and included within such express grant as proper and necessary." [25]

Nixon was not an antiparty man. In the past he had campaigned for Republican candidates when other national leaders had refused. But as President, he concluded that he owed the party faithful very little. He had determined after his unsuccessful (except in the case of Republican Charles Goodell's defeat by the Conservative party candidate, James Buckley) intervention in the 1970 congressional campaign that there was no reason he should care about the political composition of an ornamental body, namely Congress. He was content with many Democratic committee chairmen—James Eastland and Stennis, for example— whom he preferred over Republican candidates. His own personal anger against Democratic senators who were thorns in his side did not cause Nixon in 1972 to risk anything to defeat them, however. The recalcitrant ones who won reelection could be dealt with through intimidation by employing the FBI, IRS, and the Justice Department as agencies of harassment.

Nixon and his advisers believed that elections were won

through media manipulation (the 30- to 45-second television report), and by staged events which had no meaning except as theater. And so as President, Nixon viewed the Republican party as a shell which delivered nothing to him, neither from Congress in terms of his program, nor in votes at election time. He was concerned that polls showed him running behind Edmund Muskie in 1971–1972, and there was no evidence that the Republican party knew how to confront this political threat to Nixon. The Republican party, furthermore, was unable to help him take over the federal bureaucracy in his first term. Indeed, many bureaucrats had their own links to constituent groups and with Congress which allowed them to operate independently, or so Nixon believed, in defiance of his social and defense priorities.

Nixon favored his own inchoate political apparatus and servants because he believed that he would be able to "orchestrate" his little band with his interpretation of how one acquired and retained power. He would handle them more easily than he could manage the barons of his party and the nation, men like Rockefeller, Salvatori, Thurmond, and Scaife. Thus, early in 1972, Nixon chose the processors over the traditional Republican party apparatus to operate his second presidential campaign and to fashion his version of the second American Revolution. He had a grand conception; they would be his willing instruments and would be honed through CREEP for government service or personal use by the President. The processors, dependent men without an independent class consciousness, would cohere with the rich and powerful corporate leaders who, out of fear or interest, supported the President. Backed by police chiefs like Frank Rizzo of Philadelphia who became mayors of American cities, and by a group of generals and admirals who carried on a secret war in Cambodia with Nixon's acquiescence and insistence (and who fashioned the Huston Plan which sought to legalize break-ins, wiretaps, and massive surveillance in the name of national security), CREEP attempted its "new politics." The "new politics" were familiar in other parts of the American empire. They were the politics of manipulation, bribery, threat, assassination and war. Ironically, however, the methods of CREEP surprised the American middle and working classes who believed in the "new" Nixon of lowered voice, fumbling decency, détente, and an American flag in the suitcoat lapel.

While such a form of politics was "natural" in many client-states of the American imperium where elections have been staged events of the CIA or other American national security agencies (Greece, Guyana, Congo, Chile, Dominican Republic, South Vietnam, for examples), there was no precedent to guarantee that such a brand of politics would help the Republican party win local elections. The Republicans, in fact, did not do well in the 1972 congressional races. Funds did not seep down to local candidates. Republican party candidates were cut adrift even as they hoped and assumed they could ride the presidential tidal wave. While Nixon won by 17 million, the Republican party lost its majority of governorships, lost several senators with seniority, and just held its own in the House. (It is worth noting that the total number of votes cast for President in 1972 was less then the number cast in 1968, even though the eighteen-year-olds had won the vote by 1972. It is important to recall a primary purpose of voting: besides giving the power to act to a particular office seeker, it "is an implied acceptance of the general order of the State." [26])

By contrast to the Republican party's failure, CREEP was a staggering success. Maurice Stans, who ran the Finance Committee to Re-elect the President, had raised $75 million in legal and illegal contributions. Monies freely given or extorted were used only as an instrument for the President's purposes in strengthening control from the top; although from time to time, funds

were given to a few of Nixon's and Agnew's friends when it was
necessary to protect their acolytes. As it turned out, the largess
was poisoned. One Republican congressman from Maryland who
secretly took campaign funds from CREEP committed suicide
when this funding connection was discovered. Kalmbach, Dean,
Ehrlichman, and Stans used campaign funds for the Watergate
seven—and this also backfired. (Ironically, they seemed unable to
find a way to use the funds of the CIA—the king's men—to pay for
the Watergate burglary.) When Senator George McGovern
charged that Nixon's administration was the most corrupt in
American history, Nixon said it was "not necessary for me to
respond." [27]

Such concerns were considered by Nixon to be quite pic-
ayune. He knew how others governed, from Stalin to Brezhnev,
from Roosevelt to Johnson. The thought that he would be denied
the tools of a State leader—spilling the blood of others, bribery,
lies, and accumulation of private wealth—was quite unfathoma-
ble. Notable philosophers like Hegel who glorified the State have
taught that leaders are exempt from moral obligations if they are
great enough. Why should it have been otherwise for Nixon?
When men become world leaders, their reference group and their
purpose change. Dostoevsky and Charlie Chaplin understood
how people's perceptions of leaders change, and how the leaders
themselves change as they come to develop new standards which
are outside those by which men are ordinarily judged. Napoleon
was a world leader because of the murders he caused, but Raskolnikov's murders made him a mere criminal. Nixon was neither
Raskolnikov nor Monsieur Verdoux. He saw himself in a different class, a class that was peopled by the greats: de Gaulle, Stalin,
Roosevelt, Mao, Churchill and Wilson.

Following the 1972 election, President Nixon purged his own
government and carried out his will through the Executive clique

that had managed his reelection. He had said that in the second terms, administrations tend to "run out of steam . . . and usually coast downhill." He believed that "the only way that historical pattern can be changed is to change not only some of the players, but also some of the plays, if I may use the analogy to sports. . . . So, I think you can expect the next administration to be one that will have some new players. We will have some new plays, although we will consider it to be not a game, but very, very serious public business." [28] He prepared for a series of confrontations with the Congress, his own party (which now openly despised Nixon's retainers), the bureaucracy, and anyone who stood in the way of his game plan.

Like some Presidents before him, Nixon believed his power to rule was limited only by his appetites. He had hoped that the federal government would speak solely to and through him to express the National Will. In other words, the Executive would develop a series of decisions and directives solely on his reasoned or "unreasoned" judgment. The problem for any President is that the formal mechanism to enforce his purpose, the governmental bureaucracy, is sluggish. Government officials bend, but not easily, to a President. The bureaucracy is in part governed by its own rules and regulations through the civil service or through the standards laid out by professional associations. In addition, various government agencies, like labor or education, have powerful allies in nongovernmental institutions which they are more prone to accommodate than the President or his group—men the bureaucrats suspect might be in government today but gone tomorrow.

In modern times, this problem has been dealt with by a President having "agents" in the various departments who are assigned by the White House to watch the bureaucracy and the policy makers in a particular department. They have direct access to the President and are to report back to him on deviations from policy or acts of personal disloyalty. This system rarely achieved its purpose, however, because the bureaucracy and cabinet officials would isolate the presidential "agent" from knowing what was going on in the agency. On the other hand, ambitious but lowly bureaucrats will seek ways to get their critiques and their ideas to the White House. By so doing, they offer up themselves as the spies for the President and his staff. If the bureaucrat is found out within his agency, he is sacked or isolated.

Presidents are not immune to surveillance by the bureaucracy. Since World War II, the military developed its own system for spying on the White House and the President. President Eisenhower tried to control this spying system by formalizing and legitimating it through the planning boards of the National Security Council where each agency of the national security bureaucracy was present at all formal meetings. Each agency presented papers through the mechanism of the planning board. However, this system was not useful to a President who planned a diplomatic demarche. Nixon and Kissinger attempted to mask many of their diplomatic *and military* maneuvers from the Joint Chiefs. In response, the JCS encouraged agents at the White House to rummage through the desks of White House assistants for material on or about the President and the activities of his senior advisers. Nixon feared that he was going to be outflanked by the national security agencies and the Joint Chiefs of Staff who were intent on resisting the President's purposes. (A year later, Polish and Soviet analysts would argue that the President was surrounded by hawks and cold-war warriors who intended to destroy Nixon because of his interest in détente.)

Nixon believed that he needed a new and different executive structure to escape the spies, radicals, and civil servants. He was suspicious of the bureaucracy, its seeming independence and its "Democratic" proclivities or worse. He concluded that it was necessary to organize a silent coup to take control of the government. To Nixon, each high-level career official was a potential Alger Hiss or Daniel Ellsberg. Such bureaucratic phantoms had to be stopped. CREEP was to be the instrument for taking over the bureaucracy, making it responsive to the will of the President and, in turn, to those corporations and individuals which supported the President's personal revolution. Immediately after the election, the President purged his senior officials in the government, asking for the resignations of two thousand governmental officials.* He left hundreds of policy-making offices empty through the first year of his second term, although he filled more than a hundred jobs with CREEP agents. He also proposed executive reorganization which would downgrade the cabinet and make the bureaucracy directly accountable to him and his supercabinet in the White House.

Roy Ash, who headed the Presidential Advisory Council on Government Reorganization, and later became director of the Office of Management and Budget, worked with John Ehrlichman, the head of the Domestic Council (a group they hoped would oversee domestic policy in much the same way as the National Security Council controlled foreign policy), to bring about far-reaching changes in the federal bureaucracy. They intended to make those parts of the government that dealt with internal social control, work, and services subservient to Ehrlich-

---

* When Nixon came to power, he was reading Robert Conquest's *The Great Terror,* a history of Stalin's purges. Many thought he was continuing his anti-bolshevik line and wanted to brush up on his concerns. In fact, however, his interest seems to have been otherwise. He wanted to find out about the mechanics of purges in the twentieth century. Such is the nature of power that the powerful learn from each other the modes of keeping and extending it.

man's Domestic Council. The Domestic Council would then be able to provide "comprehensive responses to social and economic problems." It would get rid of the "piecemeal approach to solutions by separate departments and agencies." [29] According to the Ash recommendations, the old-line departments (State, Treasury, Justice, and most of Defense) would remain. The new departments and agencies were to be whittled, or swollen, to include *Human Resources* (a combination of HEW, Transportation, and Commerce Departments), *Natural Resources* (including the Atomic Energy Commission and parts of the Agriculture, Interior, and Defense Departments), *Economic Affairs* (to include parts of Commerce, Transportation, NASA, and the Federal Mediation Board), and *Community Development* (to include still other parts of Commerce and Transportation, HUD, the Small Business Adminstration, and the Office of Emergency Preparedness).

Both the theoretical intent and the practical result of the Ash recommendations were utterly to undercut the appropriations process. Thus, instead of 750 appropriations, the number would be reduced to 36. The hope of the council was that those at the highest reaches of the bureaucracy, plus the executive processors, would be able to start and stop programs at their whim or on the basis of their "expertise." This meant that the client relationship which existed on the lower levels of the bureaucracy, or commitments to particular groups and programs that might have reflected a local need, could be cut at the whim of top management. The bureaucracy would decrease its quasi-autonomous position in the domestic economy and become centralized and structured in strict pyramidal fashion along the lines of the large-scale conglomerate corporation.

However, the Ash proposal and Ehrlichman's Domestic Council misunderstood the present uses of bureaucracy. In Washington the bureaucracy is related to national and international corporations, while in the different regions of the United

States it is related to local oligarchic power and reflects, in terms of social class, the approximate interests of the local bourgeois class. Paradoxically, Nixon undertook to streamline the bureaucracy away from the sources of his own support—the lower middle and middle class—in the hope that he could centralize authority within himself and the executive offices. Because the Democratic party sees the bureaucracy as an employer of last (and first) resort, it believes in extending the bureaucracy downward so that it permeates all levels of public life. The Ash proposal attempted to cut such ties and sought to transform bureaucracy into a "problem solving" tool serving the most "rational" productive forces of the society. This undercut Nixon's own base and to a great extent the base of the Republican party which congressional leaders like Robert Griffin, Melvin Laird, John Rhodes, and Gerald Ford reflected. To overcome this problem, Ash and Frederick Malek, a White House adviser, tried to use the bureaucracy for direct campaign purposes. They practiced "maximum flexibility" with program funds. This was a power which Nixon expected to legitimate through his super reorganization.

As I have said, Nixon's domestic policies started from the principle of inoculation, believing that it was unnecessary to include the barons of the society as part of his inner group. However, in foreign affairs, Nixon proceeded from the "Democratic" principle of cooptation. Kissinger and Nixon decided to lasso the world's leaders into American imperial problems, particularly in those parts of the world where they did not believe their interests were involved. They sought to develop an international "leader class consciousness" that would be shared by oil sheikhs and communist revolutionary leaders alike, a leadership class with similar interests growing out of each one's power to control hierarchic social structures and wield military force. In Nixon's first term, Kissinger and Nixon used the occasion of ending the direct involvement of the American military in Indochina as a way to build such leadership alliances with the heads of China, Russia, and other nations. The sterile frozen quality of American foreign policy for a generation helped Nixon and Kissinger in their task. Leaders were flattered to be seen with an American President and to be anointed by the American Presidency, just as feudal barons were once flattered to be seen by the king.

For Nixon to proceed in his objectives, it was necessary to do so in secret. He believed in secret negotiations secretly arrived at between men who held the fate of millions in their hands. Highly complex and seemingly contradictory (to Americans) deals were cut. The number of people involved within the United States was kept to a handful. And the principle of national will and the identification of the people collectively and as individuals with the Leader had to be made complete so that such secret discussions could be successfully conducted. What was to be public was the applause of the international masses.

The foreign policy interventions of Nixon and Kissinger had a new and extraordinary result. It became possible to call on aid from the leaders of other nations to support the President and the secretary of state against powerful adversaries in their own nation. Kissinger, for example, erupted against the American press while in the midst of negotiations abroad. The Saudi Arabian king supported Nixon and Kissinger against significant elements of the American people.* Nixon and Kissinger called on enemies

---

* "In farewell remarks before the President left Jeddah, the king [Faisal of Saudi Arabia] expressed 'full confidence' that Mr. Nixon would succeed in removing all the 'blemishes' standing between the Arab world and the United States.

" 'But what is very important,' the king said, 'is that our friends in the United States of America themselves be wise enough to stand behind you, to rally around you, Mr. President, in your noble efforts, almost unprecedented in the history of mankind, the efforts aiming at securing peace and justice in the world.' " *New York Times*, 16 June 1974.

and clients alike to save them against their own institutions and citizenry. By this process they also invited the leadership of other nations into the presidential imperium. The world's leaders, Nixon hoped, would be involved in and dependent on the fate of the American Presidency. An American President and his secretary of state would be saved from the wrath of the American citizenry by the empire's satraps and adversaries abroad.

3 / The Passive Branch

The events and reverberations of the Indochina war and Watergate have caused the average congressman to realize the extent to which Congress has been trivialized in the modern period, and to consider how that process occurred. In several areas, Congress appears to want a restoration of the balance between itself and the Executive. It is useful for us to examine recent congressional efforts in those areas; what we shall see is their ironic failure. We shall see that even though the disastrous Indochina war may have emboldened senators and congressmen initially to seek the reassertion of their warmaking power, the difficulties of obtaining such power caused them to settle for much less. Congressmen have come to settle for courtesies paid to them because of their fatalistic sense that, in the modern state, power and decision continue to flow to the President and the Executive. The congressman is prepared to accept his hobbled condition if the President plays the game and follows etiquette and constitutional forms. As Ralph Nader has said:

> Even now, one senses that too many members of Congress are upset not by what he [Nixon] has done, nor the means by which he has done it—via usurpation—but by the inconsiderate way he has gone about it. When style is accorded such gravity, it is not long before style becomes the substance.[1]

Whether Left or Right, Republican or Democrat, members of Congress are not notably brave. They are cautious, and their ambition runs to place and privilege rather than to power for itself or power for a task or program. They are, therefore, compromising. It seldom crosses anyone's mind, least of all members of the House of Representatives, that the modern Congress could be made up of men with ambition *and* a program, men like Thaddeus Stevens of Pennsylvania who championed the rights of the slaves, pushed through three constitutional amendments on civil rights as the price of the South's return to the Union, and attempted to break the landowning aristocracy. One would not expect even the most congressionally minded person to say what Stevens told his colleagues:

> He [the President] is the servant of the people as they shall speak through Congress. Andrew Johnson must learn that he is your servant and that as Congress shall order he must obey. There is no escape from it. God forbid that he should have one tittle of power except what he derives through Congress and the Constitution.

That a first-term congressman, as in the case of Henry Clay, should make a bid for House Speaker and be successful would seem outrageous today. The average congressman seeks office and privilege, in a sense a ticket to the Big Game, hoping from time to time that he might be invited by the real players to take a swing at the ball. When Congress becomes obstreperous and its leadership cannot be coopted into the Executive's pocket, its ticket to the game is forfeited. This was the reason given by Dr. Henry Kissinger for lying to the Congress about the bombings of Cambodia: Congress could not be trusted to keep the information out of the hands of the people; and some members would, on occasion, even use such information with unestablished outsiders against the administration. Therefore, Kissinger made it clear: if Congress acted with "irresponsible" elements of the society, the Executive's curtain would be drawn shut. If secret bombings of Cambodia were a violation of law, so be it. There was little, it seemed, that the Congress could do about this presidential conceit. When it appeared that Kissinger would be successfully confronted on the issue of perjury and wiretaps he authorized of various journalists and staff, Kissinger threatened to resign. Fifty-two frightened senators lauded him, putting forward a Senate Resolution supporting and commending Kissinger's integrity.

Occupants of the modern Presidency have engaged in a process of preemption over Congress since the closing of the American frontier and the surge toward imperial responsibility. Perhaps the first institutional change of major proportions occurred with President Wilson, who sent to Congress a legislative program which he wanted it to pass.[2] Congressional committees very quickly found themselves debating the President's program, rather than one initiated by the Congress.

The basic contemporary presidential dynamic, which developed from this, may be described in the following way: the President takes a series of initiatives—whether legal or illegal, constitutional or not—which might flow from a real or a manufactured crisis. The form of his action is communicated through regulations, speeches, letters, executive orders, military orders, notices, proclamations, governmental reorganizations, appointments, and executive agreements. In response, the congressional leadership, for tactical reasons, will undercut the constitutional prerogative of Congress especially where crisis (and therefore the need to act!) is introduced as a factor by the President.* 3 Later, Congress, to save some vestige of involvement in affairs of state, attempts to regulate the scope of presidential initiative which, in and of itself, might have been unconstitutional. In its attempt to circumscribe the President's freedom of action, the Congress passes legislation which, in effect, ratifies or legitimates the President's right to do what he is doing. If the President is so disposed, he may veto the "corrective" legislation, in which case Congress is then almost always utterly frustrated in its efforts.

Through this process, Congress undercuts its own absolute grant of legal authority under the Constitution. It digs its own grave while the Executive, with congressional blessings, gathers to itself increasing amounts of power and resources of the society. This means, finally, that the framework of social priorities and laws is set unilaterally by the President. The further irony is that when an executive practice is pursued for a substantial period of time without congressional objection, the Supreme Court has held that congressional *inaction* amounts to implicit ratification.[4]

---

* For example, when Great Britain was in dire peril of losing to Hitler's Germany, President Roosevelt's counselors advised Senator Charles McNary, the minority leader, that the President was going to ask the Senate formally to sanction a trade with the British of overage destroyers in exchange for leasing rights to Greenland and the Bahamas. McNary told Roosevelt, according to Ben Cohen, his counselor, that the Senate—and he personally—would not object to the arrangement if the President did it on his own initiative. However, if Roosevelt were to present it formally, McNary said, the Senate Republicans would organize against the deal.

Congress Fights Impoundment*—
and Cannot Find the Right Words

The justifications for a presidential "right" to reshape internal domestic public spending on his own authority are not easily found in law or politics. (Until 1944, no President vetoed an appropriations bill; it was assumed by Congress and by Presidents that appropriations were the sole province of Congress, an assumption supported by the language of the Constitution.) The presidential power to reshape spending, however, comes from the nature of the American economy and the demands of American capitalism. Thus, a President who chooses to impound appropriations is more than a cranky Caligula. The modern-day American steward is expected to mediate the demands of an economy riddled with class differences of growing severity. There is a need to stimulate continuous economic "growth," particularly since the basic industrial sectors show high profits but little growth in productivity. The state, through the President, must find ways to encourage the rich and the corporations to invest through a credit system, tax write-offs, and a system of controls and supports that will keep the poor, the working, and the "middle" class quiet and indentured to consumerism and alienated work. This is accomplished through a kit of tricks. During the Kennedy Presidency, in order to entice the rich to invest, there was a bribe system—

> ... with its central provision of a 7 per cent investment tax credit, and the administrative liberalization of depreciation—both landmarks of progress in our drive to spur the modernization of our capital equipment. Together they increased the profitability of investment in new

* Impoundment is the method by which the President withholds or "reduces the amount of an appropriation approved by Congress and signed into law."

equipment by more than 20 percent. This was equivalent, in terms of incentives to invest, to a reduction in the corporate profits tax from 52 per cent to 40 per cent.[5]

To be sure, some liberals in Congress might object to a policy of bribing the rich. More likely, their objection is procedural. They want to be consulted in advance about the size of the bribe. However, the power of Congress on the economy is limited to that of "viewing with alarm." For example, the Joint Economic Committee of the Senate and House has only the power to hold hearings and issue a report on the annual report of the President's Council of Economic Advisers. The populist chairman of the House Banking and Currency Committee, eighty-year-old Wright Patman, can rail against the banks and the Federal Reserve System, but with no effect on the banks, the "Fed," or the concentration of banking power. Congress has not even given itself the power to audit the books of the Federal Reserve banks and boards.

The "bookkeepers" are in the executive branch. They are the keepers of the "numbers" and "language." Their responsibility is to advise and mystify on the basis of both. A President is caught between those advisers, businessmen, and economists who tell him that government expenditures for "social programs" cause inflation and lower investment, those who tell him that the state must manage and control prices and wages (thereby inhibiting private monopoly and alienating the very groups he depends on politically), and those advisers who tell him that the economy is on a merry-go-round. The larger the state becomes, the larger the corporations become, and vice versa. As both attempt to enlarge their function, their symbiotic relationship becomes obvious—for example, in aerospace and defense, motor-vehicle construction and the highway system, pollution and antipollution, health care and hospitals and nursing homes, energy needs for national security and oil corporations.

The five hundred largest corporations and the bureaucracy of the state, including policy advisers to the President, seek to develop plans for the control of the economy outside the Congress. One reason is that Congress confuses the debate with local needs and particular interests which may not be organized except for particular ad hoc purposes. The local interest is viewed as an interloper into the oligarchic planning process dominated by the largest economic and state interests in the society. Thus, for example, it has been held as axiomatic that tariffs should *not* be open to formal debates within Congress. Instead, Congress granted the President prior authority which means in practice that such questions are to be resolved bureaucratically. It is assumed that the largest corporate interests are more amenable as joint "partnership" and long-term planning than the local interests. As Nixon said in his 1973 Budget Message:

> . . . a momentum of extravagance is speeded by requirements created initially by legislative committees sympathetic to particular and narrow causes. These committees are encouraged more by special interest groups and by some programs than with *total* [emphasis added] federal spending and the taxes required to support that spending.[6]

The modern President is prepared to leave economic questions for decision among corporate managers, owners, and the federal bureaucracy. (From time to time, the unions may become part of the process of decision making, and so may the President's cronies.) Most Presidents are mystified by the economy and seek to avoid public discussions about it, in part because of their own ignorance. They are, therefore, only prepared to discuss economic matters in the most generalized terms: economic growth, cutting the budget, full employment, more starts in housing, raising or lowering the interest rates, and so forth.

Moreover, the President and the bureaucracy fear that their own mystifications would be exposed if they were debated against local needs. Thus, the Executive would prefer to avoid grass-roots public discussions which might lead to a redefinition of the public budget. Imagine if people in the districts held discussions to instruct Congress on what public expenditure should be and what the rate of taxation should be on the top 1,000 corporations. Imagine if the people on a congressional district basis decided whether they wanted a B-1 bomber or a community housing program. Imagine if they voted on a national usury law. The public budget might reflect the interests of local constituencies rather than those of multinational corporations and national bureaucracies.

The largest corporations would be exposed in town meetings since they are dedicated to gaining high profits either through extraction or sales, and have no commitment to any place, either local, regional, or national.

Liberal economists see social programs as a necessary component of an economic system that wastes people and resources. Their limited purpose is to ensure that those who have been chewed up by the industrial system (workers who develop industrial diseases), or abused by the growth of capitalism (highways through neighborhoods to service the automobile industry), will receive "benefits" which, to a large extent, workers themselves pay for through insurance and social security schemes. Corporations of course are happy to turn this "security" function over to the state, so that the state becomes the object of criticism when the programs go bad, rather than the corporations. Furthermore, the corporations are able to spread the costs of the "responsibilities" to the middle and working class through the taxing system. In its own right, the emergence of the modern state has, as I have said, meant the development of the State as an employer which gives benefits to the employed but which is not able, except through the tax system, to charge for its services or to set up enterprises that compete with the corporation.

Nixon and his processors did not want interference from either the bureaucracy or Congress in the appropriation process. In 1971, congressional leadership learned that the President intended to use impoundment as a method for reshaping social priorities along the lines he wished. Congress passed a defensive resolution requiring that it be informed of all impoundments. The Office of Management and Budget said this resolution implied that impoundment was historically legal and that, in effect, Congress was recognizing the right of the President to impound.[7] The Executive took this line in the face of a string of court cases which denied the President's power to impound according to *his* intent and purposes.

There is ample support for the proposition that executive departments have always treated spending levels assigned by appropriations legislation as permissive. Thus, one attorney general held that it was not mandatory to spend "to the extent that you are bound to expend the full amount if the work can be done for less."[8] Louis Fisher, in his admirable study, points out that when impoundment suits the purposes of Congress, legislators will not challenge the President's impoundment policy.[9] It will be rationalized as the presidential and constitutional attempt to execute faithfully the laws of the land in a just and wise manner.

When the Executive is pressed to justify its impoundment power legally, reference is usually made to the Anti-deficiency Acts of 1905–6. These acts were to prevent "undue expenditures in one portion of the year that may require deficiency or additional appropriations to complete the service of the fiscal year." Even with the 1950 amendments to the Anti-deficiency laws there was no cause to conclude that the President could assign funds anywhere he wanted.[10] Thus, when the modern President attempts to enforce his own legislative program and priorities—

whatever the Congress passes—and uses the impoundment mechanism for this end, purposes are being served that were not contemplated by the mundane Anti-deficiency laws. As Senator Sam Ervin pointed out,

> By impounding appropriated funds, the President is able to modify, reshape or nullify completely laws passed by the Legislative branch, thereby making legislative policy—a power reserved exclusively to the Congress. Such an illegal exercise of the power of his office violates clear constitutional provisions.[11]

President Nixon attempted to set out a priori requirements as to where funds should be spent, how they should be spent, and whether they should be spent. Indeed, he intended to direct appropriations expenditures to programs that the Congress had *not* passed or to hold in reserve funds for legislation that he would submit *in the future.*

How did such a "tradition" emerge? In recent times, the impoundment system has been used by Presidents for several purposes. Hoover used it to cut the government expenditure by 10 percent. In 1933 Roosevelt used impoundment as a method of changing the priorities of the federal government and the Congress from peacetime ones to those needed in preparation for war. Most impoundments in the postwar period have been around the issue of defense spending. For example, Truman impounded funds for various aircraft and the U.S.S. *United States,* Eisenhower for the Nike-ZEUS, and Kennedy for the B-70 bomber. Similar to the power of impoundment is the power to transfer funds from one program to another. For example, under the Lend Lease Act, President Roosevelt could transfer as much as 20 percent of the appropriations from one category to another. During the Second World War, the budget director could transfer 10 percent of the military appropriations from one category to another.

Nixon accepted this method of governance and claimed congressional legitimation of it. He intended that the administration would let the largest corporations be the modern planning mechanism without harassment from Congress or the use of controls from the federal bureaucracy. The public rationale for this behavior was put forward in his assertion that "Congress has not demonstrated a capacity for exercising full and comprehensive control of the issues"—namely, appropriations "restraint." Nixon's deputy attorney general from the Department of Justice, Joseph Sneed, advanced the argument that "the structure of Congress does not enable it to assume the executive responsibility for achieving this end. The harsh reality is that time and time again Congress has passed swollen appropriations acts and failed to levy the taxes necessary to avoid inflation." [12]

The "harsh reality" was somewhat different from the view presented by the voice of justice. Prior to his impeachment crisis, through impoundment and the elimination of many individual line items in the budget, Nixon intended to use his budget as the guide to expenditure without having to pass through the gauntlet of the Congress. The President's tastes ran to the Safeguard/ABM system, larger merchant marine fleet, supersonic transport, and the manned bomber, while he concluded that model cities, urban renewal, and health research were not in the national interest. Nixon would expend funds only on those public-works projects that were on his list of legislative priorities, not those the Congress initiated and passed.*

It was the conservative Senator Ervin who confronted Nixon on his domestic powers, from Watergate to impoundment. Ervin's bill S.373, provided that the President was required

* Nixon's consistency is not very high. Each action is to him like a play in a game. Thus, Nixon pressed for an appropriation to integrate schools. The Congress passed it. HEW then sought support from state officials who hired teachers for the programs. The administration then impounded funds, saying that they could not be spent.

... to notify each house of the Congress by special message of every instance in which he impounds or authorizes an impoundment by any officer of the United States. Each special message must specify, first, the amount of the funds impounded; second, the date on which funds were ordered to be impounded; third, the date the funds were impounded; fourth, any account, department or establishment of the Government to which the impounded funds would have been available for obligation except for the impoundment; fifth, the period of time during which funds could be impounded; sixth, the reasons for the impoundment and seventh, the estimated fiscal, economic and budgetary effects of the impoundment.

The bill further provided

that the President shall cease the impounding of funds specified in each special message unless the Congress approves the impoundment within 60 calendar days of continuous session after the message is received.[13]

Given the nature of the American economy, it was doubtful that any legislative scheme or judicial decisions would make a difference in the actions of a President who stated that his responsibility was to protect the American economic system. As strong as the Ervin bill appeared, certain problems became apparent in the course of the Senate Hearings. The President was given a sixty-day "free ride." The bill assumed that the President had the right to impound beyond the right outlined in the Antideficiency Acts. Thus, Congress legitimated the President's past actions, even as it attempted to find a series of mechanical controls to get him to follow the appropriations acts. In any case, as Roy Ash, director of the Office of Management and Budget, said, the President can choose which laws he cares to follow. The Nixon administration's rationale to Congress for not following the appropriations laws was that he had to enforce the debt ceiling passed by Congress.

The President, through exercise of his veto power, can with likely success veto almost any legislation that seems to cut into his power. As Senator Muskie said to one witness on the impound-ment bill:

> If it is strengthened in ways you have suggested, it is still legislation. It would have to be enacted by both Houses of Congress, then go to the President for signature. If it is tough effective legislation, we can expect a veto.[14]

And if it cannot override the veto, Congress appears to confirm the Executive's authority to impound. Yossarian would certainly have appreciated such a dilemma.

Nixon and any future President need hardly be concerned about impoundment legislation that attempts to limit the Presi-dent's ability to manipulate the priorities of the nation. Under the Economic Stabilization Act of 1970, the President had wide dis-cretionary powers which were undefined. He was given the power to regulate the business cycle, employment, wages, and prices. Although he said that he would not use the authority given to him by the Congress, a year went by and he decided to set up a committee system that represented the largest organized inter-ests. However, he did not set up the kind of economic controls that would limit inflation or unemployment.

In 1973 Congress gave Nixon the power to set ceilings on rents, which he refused to use. He believed that bigness, i.e., the rich, should not be penalized for their condition. No doubt he believed that the Fortune-500 corporations would identify him as the institution of the Presidency itself, rather than a mere occu-pant. Thus, he thought that they would come to his rescue in his battles with Congress and the courts. This was not an irrational conclusion since Congress had further authorized the President (in other words, the largest corporations) to act as he saw fit because of the crisis of the economy. Nixon had already used the 1970 act as his primary instrument in fashioning and mediating the economy. His fashion was not a very happy one for the bulk of the people. But such criticism could merely mean that he was not a benevolent dictator. Congress, as an institution, fought to remain in the game of state power as a junior partner of the President by surrendering its own power to shape the economy. Nixon's problem was that he did not know how to "manage" the economy.

The national leadership class, the barons, are of course comfortable with administrative management of the economy. The barons believe in the abstractions of the bureaucracy and the university in economics and politics where national interest and purpose are not grounded in anything except an ambiguous ideal. Keynesians have taught in the universities that the corporations can be persuaded or forced to act with the bureaucracy in the "national interest." Once the mask is torn away, however, the audience finds that such abstract ideals end up servicing the economic and status interests of the military, administrative, and corporate elites.

There remained the theme of congressional involvement in shaping priorities for the nation. What was to become of the legislation, should it pass, if impoundment could be invoked by a President? Ervin's last term in the Senate was during the Watergate Congress, the 93rd. It seemed unlikely that many liberals or conservatives would continue the battle for anti-impoundment legislation because it was unenforceable and would have a dialectically opposite result. One former liberal adviser to President Kennedy, Theodore Sorensen, had even passed the word that impoundment was an executive prerogative.[15] And conservatives also believed that the economy required presidential discretion.

The barons and economists saw this power as an important tool in the executive kit to help or hurt particular groups and classes.

Congress Tries to Take Back
the Warmaking Powers

As we have seen, whether a leader is a tyrant or a virtuous democratic statesman, he must find sources of legitimacy for his actions. Even if the action stems from emergency or necessity, the question of constitutional legitimacy in the minds of people becomes a crucial psychological ingredient which a leader must find if he is to enlist support from the people. When the southern states seceded from the Union, a casus belli was necessary to begin a war that would restore the United States to political and legal union. Lincoln tied several clauses of the Constitution together to rationalize actions that would restore the principle of union and, in the process, rally the northern and border citizenry to the Union's cause.

President Lincoln combined the commander-in-chief clause of the Constitution with the phrase that it was the duty of the President "to take care that the laws be faithfully executed." Through these clauses Lincoln derived the "war power." In the period between the fall of Fort Sumter and the special session of Congress, Edward Corwin points out, Lincoln proclaimed a blockade, called up 81,000 soldiers and sailors, spent several millions from the treasury unauthorized by Congress, closed off the Post Office Service to "treasonable correspondence," suspended the writ of habeas corpus in certain geographic areas, and caused the arrest of at least 13,000 people contemplating "treasonable practices." Lincoln expected Congress to ratify these activities after the fact.[16]

Thus, Lincoln developed the presumption that the power of

the Presidency acting alone was sufficient to prosecute a total war in defense of the Union. The actions Lincoln took in the context of the breakup of the United States are the ground upon which his successors stand when they approach real or imagined dangers. Presidents invoke the principles of survival, national security, inherent power, and national emergency for events and situations that may be initiated by the Executive itself. Yet they no longer have an air of legitimacy about them.

I have intimated that when a modern President states that his actions are taken in the name of emergency or national security, the citizen should be forewarned. It means that the Executive is reaching to fill spaces of power which hitherto have been left either undefined by the Constitution, have been shared between the different branches of the government, or were originally the spaces of *individual* citizens or citizens in voluntary association with one another.

When a President or the State undertake to fill all the spaces, an immediate problem arises for the citizen. If a President says that an emergency exists, it is important to ask for which interest, class, or section of the nation. The power of the President and a bureaucracy to create categories within which others must live is manifested when he states that there is an emergency or a "threat" to the United States. The psychological need for belief and authority will cause large numbers of people, being pliant, to conclude that such an emergency exists and that they should act accordingly.

As President Lincoln demonstrated, a President may *intend* to act contrary to statute and the Constitution. This may reach absurd proportions, as in the case of Nixon where no democratically defined emergency exists to justify his actions. For example, in defense of the plumbers, Nixon's outfit claimed that for reasons of national security, the President had the power to order breaking-and-entering teams into the offices of citizens to obtain their property or the property of third parties. (It should be noted that breaking-and-entering teams, without benefit of judicially approved order, were formally part of the FBI until 1966.)[17]

While it may be of little solace to the individual citizen, there is ample precedent for the principle that a President is not able to detain citizens or to take their property unless the Congress has given express authorization to act accordingly. Even in time of war, according to one Supreme Court case *(Brown* v. *United States)*, the President is not able to order confiscation on his own authority.[18]

When Congress acts as an independent body, some politicians and scholars have made a creditable argument that the State, through statute, should have the right to detain citizens when a war is declared. But when Congress itself is reduced to nothing but an applauding section for an Executive that has already acted, then the entire process of separated powers and balanced government becomes farcical. In such a situation, the Congress is reduced to a bunch of lobbyists and cheerleaders begging for the Executive's favors—and the citizen had better learn to fend for himself. Most members of Congress are as unconnected to the unorganized and the unseen as are the executive clique and any President who is anointed by the "barons and the party."

The beginnings of citizen involvement that emerged during the Johnson period—through such quaint ideas as the maximum feasible participation of the poor in public decisions—frightened the constituted authority of both Congress and the Presidency. Such programs, which called forth a chance, however negligible, for the wretched and the unorganized to act like citizens rather than wards of the state, were viewed by Nixon and Congress as changing the basis of social and property relationships among the people. For members of Congress, this posed a dilemma. Their legitimacy was under attack from all sides. It seemed to some that Congress had to move toward the people or take its place next to the White House as an impeached institution. And since the question of legitimacy is crucial to those who wield power, the question remained: "From whence does legitimacy stem?"

The twentieth century offers two choices to Americans who are interested in political legitimacy. Once God is no longer the grantor of a state's legitimacy, it most likely has to devolve from the people. This means a redistribution of power to the people, a redefinition of what additional rights the people obtain through citizenship, and a change in the very nature of what it means to be united and a state. Alternatively, legitimacy could devolve from a Constitution; a document which in the American case had long since fallen into desuetude in those areas having to do with balances and checks between the branches of the government, or with powers and rights reserved to the people. In practice, neither principle of legitimacy was followed. Instead the President was chosen to act for a System which did not care to look too closely at the roots of its legitimacy. An operational legitimacy was adopted by a President who saw himself acting for the System. In this capacity the President and his immediate staff, agencies, or the bureaucracy write into law, on the basis of national security or emergency, justifications for actions already taken. They succeed in weaving a quilt of illegal and legal principles which cannot easily be unthreaded. Congress is then reduced to rationalizing such behavior which the interpreters of the law, who have operating powers, take on their own initiative. The bulk of Congress accepts the principle of "emergency" because its members have come to believe that they are constituted authority, holding legitimacy not through the people or an eighteenth-century Constitution, but through their identification with established institutions of which the President is the recognized leader and arbiter.

From 1968, Congress was peppered with demands from individuals and interest groups to act to stop the war. The cost of the Indochina war seemed greater than the benefits; and Congress wondered whether the President had sufficient support to continue the war, or had a "secret plan" to end it. The party of the imperium, the Democratic party, wanted a restoration of congressional power. Its leaders believed that the brokering function needed to be shared between the Congress and the President to maintain order within the United States. (The record shows that imperialists would have risked very little by such a political concurrence between the Executive and Congress.) Because of the Indochina war, however, the Executive's power to make war came under attack with a certain unrelenting quality, even from those who ordinarily favored a strong Executive. Nicholas Katzenbach, who had argued as undersecretary of state that the President had unlimited power to make war on his own initiative, maintained in 1973 that a "real national emergency should be one in which the President and the Congress concur." [19] Other traditional roles were reversed. Senator Barry Goldwater, who promoted himself as a believer in limited government—including checks and balances—fought against those in Congress who attempted to reassert congressional power to declare war. He correctly pointed out that little wars were not "a phenomenon new to the national experience." [20] While Congress from time to time had attempted to put restraints on the President's power to engage the forces of the United States in war, it almost never succeeded. Goldwater pointed out that there have been dozens of attempts to "shackle" a President's interventionary penchant. All have been unsuccessful.

For example, in 1912, Senator Augustus Bacon proposed an amendment to an army appropriations bill that would have prohibited the use of military funds by the Executive beyond the jurisdiction of the United States. This amendment was defeated—the United States had already decided to be a great world power. It had one of the five largest military budgets in the world, so the chance that such an amendment would carry was virtually nil. The best that Congress could hope to attain was Hiram

Johnson's successful resolution after the First World War which instructed the President to keep the Congress informed about the American military intervention in Siberia.

Between 1922 and 1928, there were further attempts to control the disposition of military forces. Each sought to undercut the American imperial role. Senators such as David S. King of Utah and Kenneth McKellar of Tennessee objected to the practice of supporting U.S. armed forces as a collection agent for the bankers and corporations in the Dominican Republic, Haiti, or Nicaragua. Historians do not adequately report the massive social democratic attempts by the American middle class and part of its working class to control or stop imperialism. The anti-imperialist torch was carried in the 1920s with considerable success by Robert M. La Follette, Sr., of Wisconsin and Burton K. Wheeler of Montana. In 1924, they were the standard bearers of the Progressive party and received nearly 5 million votes in the presidential election. (John Davis, the Wall Street representative, campaigned on the Democratic party ticket *for* imperialism but against corruption and malfeasance; Calvin Coolidge, an earlier version of Gerald Ford, campaigned on normalcy, common sense, the Founding Fathers, the Constitution, *and* imperialism.) In 1928, Senator John Blaine of Wisconsin continued the anti-imperial argument that American forces should not be used for intervention "unless war has been declared by Congress or unless a state of war actually exists under recognized principles of international law." Yet, all such attempts at limitation failed when they were put to the vote in Congress.

Since 1940, Congress's legislative attempts to control the presidential penchant for warmaking have been usually ignored and repeatedly violated by Presidents. President Franklin Roosevelt violated two neutrality laws when he ordered the navy to convoy military supplies for Britain and Russia. He also sent American draftees to Iceland and Greenland, in direct violation of the Selective Service Act which stated that draftees were not to be employed outside the Western Hemisphere. Throughout the last years of the Indochina war, congressional intent was consistently violated. In 1970 and 1971 the Congress passed amendments to an assistance act which forbade the use of troops in Laos and Cambodia. Each of the amendments was violated and ignored by the President. The Congress adopted the Mansfield Amendment to the Military Selective Service Act, declaring that it was the "policy of the United States" to terminate all U.S. military operations in Indochina at the earliest practicable date and to provide for the prompt and orderly withdrawal of all United States military forces. However, when Nixon signed the bill into law, he stated that he intended to ignore the policy written into law by Congress.

Congress persisted nonetheless. In 1970, the Senate Foreign Relations Committee and House Foreign Affairs Committee developed a variety of bills and resolutions on war powers. In 1973, after the apparent termination of the Indochina war, the Congress passed several versions of a war powers bill. Senator Jacob Javits explained the purpose of his legislation:

> We live in an age of undeclared war, which has meant Presidential war. Prolonged engagement in undeclared, Presidential war has created a most dangerous imbalance in our Constitutional system of checks and balances.
> . . . [The bill] is rooted in the words and the spirit of the Constitution. It uses the clause of Article 1, Section 8 to restore balance which has been upset by the historical disenthronement of that power over war which framers of the Constitution regarded as the whole Article of Congressional power—the exclusive authority of Congress to "declare war"; the power to change the nation from a state of peace to a state of war.[21]

The Senate Foreign Relations Committee objected to the notion that the President could make foreign obligations on his own initiative, including the use of the armed forces for war. The committee seemed uninterested in the cooptive principle of merely "drawing Congress into the decision-making process insofar as he [the President] finds it useful and convenient."[22] Rather, the intent of members of Congress was to ensure that, in the future, no Congress would be able to vote a blank check Gulf of Tonkin type of resolution without being bound by the War Powers resolution reasserting congressional power of initial declaration.

Under the terms of the Senate resolution, the President's use of the armed forces was confined to repelling an attack against the United States, forestalling such an attack where it appears to be imminent, repelling or forestalling an attack against American forces abroad, evacuating U.S. citizens located in foreign countries, and carrying out specific statutory authorizations that are not to be inferred from other treaties or appropriations. In reporting out the resolution, the Senate committee stated that it intended to provide protection "to the American people" in the era of undeclared presidential wars by

> requiring that the Congress as well as the President must
> participate in the critical decision to authorize the use of the
> Armed Forces of the United States, our armed forces
> abroad, or upon U.S. citizens abroad in defined
> circumstances. It provides as much flexibility as the wit and
> ingenuity of the President and Congress may be jointly
> capable of constructing.[23]

The Senate War Powers bill further attempted to make clear that no bilateral Security treaty is self-executing, meaning that authorization for any introduction of armed forces was to be obtained from Congress. Further, the President was to report any use of armed forces "promptly" in writing to both houses of Congress. He was required to give a "full account of the circumstances under which he has acted—the estimated scope of such hostilities or situations, and the consistency of the introduction of such forces with the War Powers bill."

According to the Senate report, Section 5 is "the crucial embodiment of Congressional authority in the war powers field based on the mandate of Congress enumerated so comprehensively in Article 1, Section 8 of the Constitution." Section 5 stated that armed action taken on the President's initiative shall not be sustained beyond thirty days from the date of the introduction of such armed forces unless (1) the President determines and certifies to the Congress in writing "that unavoidable military necessity" makes it impossible to disengage because such disengagement would endanger the safety of U.S. armed forces, (2) that Congress is physically unable to meet, or (3) the use of such forces has been authorized in specific legislation by the Congress.

The appearance achieved through the War Powers bill is that of responsible legislators attempting again to exercise their constitutional responsibilities with Congress as a whole attempting to restore its authority in the area of war and peace. They thought that such a restoration would patch up the system of checks and balances which, in turn, would give rise to independent and dispassionate inquiry on the part of Congress. Thus the rights of the citizen would be protected. As Justice John Marshall Harlan, a former Wall Street lawyer, had said, the citizen's rights were dependent on the check and balance system.

Political support for the War Powers bill was wide ranging. Men who, just a decade before, had arrogated enormous power to themselves and to the President were now saying that the executive authority should be limited. Now removed from the center of power, they spoke of the necessity of defining the powers of the President more carefully—they saw their own class separated from the sources of executive power as, individually, they became the stewards of major American institutions. Nicholas Katzenbach was now the vice-president of IBM. In 1967, he had said that the Gulf of Tonkin resolution was a "functional equivalent" of a war declaration; in 1973, he testified in favor of the congressional restoration of its war power. McGeorge Bundy, head of the Ford Foundation, testified for the bill, saying that it was needed and that, in any case, it would not have sharply affected "the essential processes of the Cuban missile crisis."

There were doubts about the War Powers bill. Some congressmen said that it gave the President authority which he formerly did not have and legitimated activities which the Congress and the Constitution had not approved. Senator James Abourezk of South Dakota pointed out that the legislation simply abandoned "the constitutional requirement that no war be entered without *prior* Congressional declaration." [24] The problem with Abourezk's view was that *this "right" already existed.* It was the cornerstone of the American imperial system. Under 10 USC 712, the President "upon the application of the country concerned" could "detail" members of the armed forces for military purposes in

(1) any republic in North America, Central America or South America; (2) the Republic of Cuba, Haiti or Santo Domingo; (3) during a war or a declared national emergency, any other country that he considers it advisable to assist in the interest of national defense.

Furthermore, any member of the armed forces, "subject to the prior approval of the Secretary of the military department concerned," could "accept any office from the country to which he is detailed, as if serving with the armed forces of the United States." * The War Powers legislation did nothing to correct this law of the empire.

* Those familiar with the operations of imperialism know that the requests for military aid are written in either the U.S. Department of Defense or Department of State.

Yet it is too broad a generalization to say that law was only a rationalized system for the protection of an expansionist empire. In fact, the early American law was meant to hold in check the expansionists and adventurers. It was recognized in law that a foreign policy of noninvolvement and neutrality was crucial to the new state. Enormous care was taken *not* to endanger relations with foreign princes or states "with whom the United States are at peace." Behavior that endangered peaceful relations was adjudged by Congress to be a "high misdemeanor punishable by a fine not to exceed three thousand dollars nor the term of imprisonment be more than three years."[25] Aaron Burr was tried under this statute. Furthermore, "high misdemeanor" was a term which, when applied to a President in office, could translate into an impeachable offense.

The fact that Nixon and Kissinger carried out a war (against Cambodia) while lying to another branch of government, stating that they were not doing so, would have been enough to impeach Nixon according to the intention of the first Congresses. The modern development of paralegal activity has meant that the ruler coopts much of the bureaucracy and funds of the state in criminal enterprises, surrounding them with the appearance of legality. Thus, Nixon made war secretly; but so had others since 1940. The purpose of the early laws was to stop officials or private citizens from making war on their own, either in the scope of their position as government officials or as private citizens. This 1794 law and its updated version were applicable against modern Presidents if the will were there to apply it. But times had changed, it was argued; the empire required a different set of norms and laws, presumably fashioned by the Executive.

Senator J. William Fulbright, a powerful minority on his committee, was uneasy about the War Powers legislation because it reinforced executive prerogative. He wondered whether Congress was, in fact, writing into its toughest legislation to control presidential power the right of the President to initiate a preemptive attack on another nation. As Fulbright said, the

> provision authorizing the President to "forestall direct and imminent threat" of an attack could also be used to justify actions such as the Cambodian intervention of 1970 and the Laos intervention of 1971, both of which were explained as necessary to forestall attacks on American forces.[26]

Furthermore, the President still retained the power to use nuclear weapons first on his own initiative at any time. Fulbright favored the House version of the War Powers bill, although he disagreed with the part of the House's version which gave the President 120-days' grace period to make war on his own.

The House bill gave the President "maximum flexibility" in the opening stages of the undeclared war. The Executive enjoyed the conceit that it had to "respond immediately to emergencies," as a Justice Department assistant said. But the problem for the people was that the Executive did not react to so much as *initiate* crises. Some reasoned that the President and the military were given a 60-day free ride to make war. The bill which finally emerged from the Congress, House Joint Resolution 542, called for a cutoff of Presidential war after 60 days unless the Congress extended it. The President vetoed the bill, saying that

> We may well have been unable to respond the way we did during the Berlin crisis of 1961, the Cuban missile crisis of 1962, the Congo rescue operation in 1964, and the Jordanian crisis of 1970—to mention just a few examples.[27]

Nixon was especially "disturbed" by the fact that "No overt Congressional action would be required to cut off those [Presidential warmaking] powers; they would disappear automatically unless the Congress extended them."[28] In other words, it was a reversal of the usual situation wherein if Congress did nothing, or was split, the President could carry on his policies and activities.

Within forty-eight hours of vetoing the War Powers bill, President Nixon ordered an alert for all American forces around the world. The alert, in the midst of the Middle East crisis, was widely interpreted as an attempt to take the mind of the nation from the firings and resignations at the Department of Justice. More likely, it was related to the President's views as expressed in his message vetoing the War Powers resolution. In his veto, he had said the passage of the bill

> would, for example, strike from the President's hand a wide range of important peace keeping tools by eliminating his ability to exercise quiet diplomacy by subtle shifts in our military deployments.

Nixon's alert did not immediately intimidate Congress. For the first time, it overrode Nixon on an important issue, even though the victory was with little content: the President could still make war on his own initiative. And so Lincoln's constitutional ideas of war powers were legitimated by Congress even as Congress attempted to cut them back.

Is it the case that all branches of the government are diseased, and that none sees itself, structurally, as part of the people? Could Congress be something other than an appendage of the President, the corporations, the military, and the bureaucracy? Could it develop natural antibodies and "warning systems" to revitalize the body politic? Could it identify with the people, or is it doomed to be a part of the state, requiring the people to retain rights *against* the will of Congress? If the latter is the case, must we conclude that neither Congress nor the President can function *with* the people?

Take the scourge of war. Executive foreign and military policies invariably bring the people and Congress to the brink of war. Suppose forms are followed and a President asks for a declaration of war:

> Once the war declaration is demanded, the managers of the State have already deceived the people and the legislators. If the Congress were to deny the Executive and his bureaucracy a requested declaration of war, once it was requested, the Executive would be in a position of a band of thieves who up to that point had engaged in criminal enterprise. They would have to be stopped, but who would stop them? And where would the alternate source of legitimacy and power to the Executive government be found? If the answer is "the people", then the nation and society are set immediately on a revolutionary course. For its purposes the Executive merely requires complicity from Congress, not agreement. Members of Congress will comply rather than risk internal revolution to stop a war abroad. As a result of [such] Congressional compliance, the Executive is able to transform war into the Zeitgeist of the State . . . and thereby is justified in shedding the people's blood.[29]

Is there no other way?

The Congress's power to make war is itself limited, according to Chief Justice Taney. The genius of the American government, in his view, was to be peaceful, and not to wage war for conquest, aggrandizement, acquisition or aggression. This could only mean that the people retain those rights to resist both executive usurpation of power and congressional acquiescence to frolics of war or militarism. If Congress does intend to break the habit of deriving its existence and legitimacy from the established sources of power (the military, local economic oligarchs, the police, and some labor leaders), then congressional members must find their legitimacy in the people who will act as citizens to determine their interests and purposes in confrontation with the present corporate structures. It has been the debilitating war in

Indochina and the people's reaction to it that has given Congress a chance to redefine its relationship to the Executive and the people. Finding legitimacy in the people will mean that Congress will have to develop an antagonistic stance to imperialism and war because of their pathological qualities. I suggest in a later Note a mechanism that could initiate the process of popular legitimacy from the people as a whole, rather than from either the individual or his corporate-military extensions.

4 / Nixon's
/ Watergate

The dogged work of Bob Woodward and Carl Bernstein, two young investigative reporters for the *Washington Post*, kept the fires of Watergate burning throughout the 1972 campaign. Most of the press, however, gave little or no coverage to the story and concentrated instead on the weaknesses of George McGovern, thus protecting Nixon from any hard media scrutiny. Yet the rumors about CREEP persisted. McGovern denounced the Nixon administration as the most corrupt in history, but it was hard for McGovern to make his case. Both readers and reporters alike, it seemed, had become inured to scandal and institutional crime. Terror bombings, secret invasions, government deals with large corporations for their own profit, and petty stealing were the stuff of daily news on the back pages. It was not until after Nixon was safely elected that the processors of CREEP began to make headlines and to receive massive television coverage. The revelations, the White House coverup, and daily "confessions" from the broken processors caused Congress to begin serious consideration of impeachment. Nixon was surprised at the outcry and responded by venting his own outrage against the media. He knew the media had greatly favored him during the 1972 campaign by allowing him to "disappear" from the campaign itself. But he also knew that the vengeance of the journalists would be great because they had been tricked by the White House press office, inoculated against investigation.*

Nixon felt maligned about Watergate. He had done little more than what others before him had done. It is beyond the scope of this essay to discuss the various revelations and White House responses. These have all been well documented in the newspapers and by congressional committees. What is important to note in the labyrinthine maze of Watergate are the outlines of the System itself. Was it "working"? Some said that Nixon's survival would mean there were no limits that could be placed on him or on future Presidents. Others said that the limp punishment of Nixon's group for their wrongdoing was proof that this was a nation of "laws not men." Some interpreted the President's performance as an act of will against other men and institutions which themselves showed no will or tactical ability to survive. They believed that no group was prepared to challenge Nixon directly. No opposing individual, clique, or institution had mass legitimacy and, therefore, Nixon would remain President. But Nixon was in for a personal storm.

Political leaders view themselves as skillful if they know when to take a risk or espouse a cause in order to obtain a desired result. Skill for a political leader is wrapped up in "timing." Nixon continued to manage and gauge all aspects of the Watergate

* Nixon himself had never learned the media's weakness for status. The cynics in Washington believed that the entire Watergate affair could have been avoided by "backgrounders" for the media people during Nixon's years in office.

scenario after March 1973, but his timing was off. He believed from the beginning that his strongest card was to wait things out. He would obfuscate issues, tie up the courts, and slow down legal processes wherever possible. Nixon sought to vaccinate the opposition and believed that if an hors d'oeuvre were offered and eaten, the claimant would skip the main course. Aides, cohorts, tapes, and transcripts were to be fed to the courts, the media, and the public a piece at a time. He thought he could "pierce the boil" by releasing the tapes. But he reacted too slowly, never finding a way to fashion *the* dramatic act which would divert the lens and change the frame from Watergate. He allowed the process to become inexorable.

After the Watergate break-in and the failure of the White House cover story, it appeared that Spiro Agnew would play an important role in Nixon's troubles. During his first term, Agnew had developed a solid "in depth" political constituency. When a politician has "in depth" support it means that he is able to give explanations, without proof, to his supporters. A clever politician hones his explanations by striking a pose that touches the psychological needs of his constituency. For Vice-President Agnew, this meant effecting a righteous demeanor and giving speeches calculated to support meritocracy and authoritarianism. In four years he had learned to speak with a proper amount of gravitas, affecting the tone of a stern paternalist delivering verbal spankings, and more, to an establishment which had become slothful, permissive, and soft. Some thought of him as incorruptible. He had begun a series of high-level discussions with right-wing intellectual luminaries, including Irving Kristol and Herman Kahn. He seemed to be prepping himself for the Presidency.

As the vice-president, Agnew interested himself in two groups as his constituency. One was the low-paid civil servant of the bureaucracy who received his salary (and then pension) for processing those more wretched than the bureaucrat. Another group included the small property owner, the shopkeepers, and local entrepreneurs who accepted the pyramidal order and admired those international businessmen, scufflers who were on top of the pyramid. Had Agnew become President, his personal clique would have included the arriviste millionaires (Thomas Pappas, Frank Sinatra, and Clement Stone), although his personal and financial base would have remained the Maryland builders and entrepreneurs, men who had done so much to turn the living and natural spaces around Washington and Baltimore into staging areas for the highway system.

At first, the media thought that Agnew would benefit from the Watergate misfortunes. But it turned out that Agnew was neither a help nor a hindrance to Nixon. Early in 1973, Agnew distanced himself from the Watergate issue, giving only perfunctory interviews and statements to the media. Some thought it was because Agnew was genuinely disgusted with the "bunch of clowns" who were involved in the Watergate break-in. Others thought Agnew did not want to help a President who seemed to have ordered his White House staff to shun him publicly at every opportunity.

There was another reason, however. Agnew knew of his own Achilles' heel in Maryland. He could not be a rhetorical warrior lest he find himself facing embarrassing questions about a grand jury investigation into Maryland political graft. Confronted with the low esteem in which he was held at the White House, knowing he would have to separate himself from the quicksand around Watergate, and yet hoping some gain could fall his way, Agnew sent others to speak for him. Victor Gold, his former press secretary, pounced on the "foolishness and stupidity" of the Watergate characters.

While Agnew's supporters pictured the White House staff and Nixon as unprincipled fools and bunglers, there was an advantage for Nixon in the Agnew affair. The White House knew that there was a "cancer" around the vice-presidency. Through Charles Colson, whose law firm had become Agnew's unofficial advisers, Agnew's bribery and extortion problem was known to the White House at the beginning of Nixon's second term. After John Dean switched sides on Watergate, problems for Agnew rapidly grew to gigantic proportions. The Justice Department bureaucrats did not want to have someone who had been named a thief in grand jury proceedings to become the acting President, or President—both of which were distinct possibilities, given the pressure on Nixon to resign because of corruption.

On the other hand, the White House advisers hoped that forcing the resignation of Agnew and breaking his epaulets of power in public would reduce the chances of attack on Nixon. They believed that congressional leaders would reason that the System could not take the shock of Nixon's decapitation if Agnew were sacrificed to the crowd. Agnew seemed to be the meat which would have to be thrown to keep Nixon on the throne. A leader must find sacrificial goats to quiet the mob or he must find a false leader who can for a short period of time take the angry mob's eyes from him. It was Nixon's hope that anxiety and docility would overtake the people and Congress if enough leaders, advisers, and processors were sacrificed. Since Agnew had been the symbol of the right-wing authoritarian, however, his removal had to be accomplished with care. It was important not to arouse Agnew's slumbering constituency or hold it up to ridicule, a process that would have occurred had there been a trial or impeachment of Agnew. If Agnew could be removed deftly, Nixon could placate Congress with an appointment of one of its own. With the aid of the establishment's man, Elliot Richardson, Nixon arranged the quiet excision. But neither Agnew's removal nor his replacement greatly helped the President.

When Nixon chose Gerald Ford as his new vice-president, with ruffles and flourishes, he intended to accomplish several objectives. Nixon believed that Ford was a close friend and loyal to him. They had worked together in Washington since the 1940s, supporting the Republican party position on anticommunism, heavy defense spending, heavy subsidization to the capitalist class, while insisting on "balanced" budgets. Nixon liked Ford's politics and intended to convince Congress that with this appointment, he was returning to the symbolic forms, nodding in the direction of congressional etiquette (stroking) and "restoring" the principle of an executive-congressional partnership.

Through the Ford appointment, Nixon hoped to appeal to the people who were Republicans "by nature," people who generally accept authority as it is, believing in the innate goodness of the small town and the American dream, while supporting corporate plunder under the guise of individual initiative and "ingenuity." Just as in the Kennedy administration advisers were chosen because they had been junior fellows at Harvard, Nixon admired Ford because he had been an all-American football player—showing, supposedly, that he could take the hard knocks of politics. The military was pleased with Ford's appointment since he was known as a strong supporter of military expenditures, whatever they might be, never shirking from bellicose actions. Ford had once said in 1961 that President Kennedy should be given authority to call up one million men on his own whim so that he would have a "big stick" to shake in the face of Khrushchev.[1] Ford had, of course, supported the twists and turns of the American war in Indochina. At the same time, he was "tolerated" by politicians because he was neither wise nor particularly sneaky, although by the spring of 1974 the latter characterization was debatable. As vice-president, Ford adopted a "multi-opt" strategy: he would both criticize and support Nixon, while leaving to Fortune and Fate whether he himself would become President. Ford wanted the President to tell all, to release the tapes. He wondered out loud about who would be in his cabinet and he questioned the ability of the President to negotiate with the Soviets.

Ford's position in the nation seemed to be stronger than Nixon had anticipated. Through continuous speechmaking, Ford urged the Republican party to rally behind its principles of narrow self-interest and restricted class privilege. Politically, he wanted the Republican party to forget about Watergate and Nixon and to remember the narrow principles upon which the Republicans based their actions. Ford maneuvered himself into a primary position within the Republican party through cross-country preachings on the sins of omission and commission called Watergate. In one speech, Ford made a direct bid for military support, saying that the President was being placed in a precarious position in his discussions with the Soviets and that the United States was in a weakened condition because of the President's handling of Watergate.[2] The President wondered whether Ford was not tiring himself by all his travels.

While Nixon's appointment of Ford enabled Ford to cement his own relationship with the Republican party, the appointment did nothing for the party itself, as the special congressional elections in 1974 indicated. The benefits to Nixon, therefore, were marginal at best. The Republican party began to see in Ford an alternative, someone who would not patronize his fellow Republicans with contemptuous dares. Nixon had said:

> Don't assume the time to run for an office is only when it is a sure thing. Show me a candidate who is not a hungry candidate, show me a candidate who isn't willing to take a risk and risk all, even risk losing, and I will show you a lousy candidate.[3]

Nixon saw politics as a poker game in which people were chips to bet, sacrifice, or risk. Once a crisis occurred, however, all bets seemed to be off. John Dean let it be known that he would not be a scapegoat. The Agnew disgrace was accompanied by successive resignations and indictments. The younger processors went first, then those farther up in the hierarchy. The President's coterie split asunder, each attempting to protect himself—thereby further isolating the President. The problem for Nixon was that he needed his coterie intact because he had ignored the development of the Republican party. He had failed to use the process of cooptation (familiar to the Democrats) which would have shared power with different interests and which would, therefore, have made it more likely that different interest groups would have come to his defense.

The reader might ask whether there was any way that Nixon could have been helped or could have avoided the decimation of himself and his "outfit." In other words, could he have saved himself through virtue in the Machiavellian sense? A man endowed with Machiavellian virtue might have quickly admitted formal responsibility for the Watergate break-in and would immediately have been forgiven, on rationalizations ranging from national security to pranksterism. To do so, Nixon would have had to endow the action with his own name. He had to say that he ordered the break-in. His psychological inability to do so, either out of embarrassment or political fear, or guilt, utterly miscalculated the current American mood in which the most powerful are forgiven the most heinous activities if they quickly admit doing them.

There are massive flaws in Nixon as a man. He was filled with paranoid rage, overly insecure, and secretive. Perhaps these flaws caused him to misunderstand his public role—how to act as President. For example, Nixon surrounded himself with a group of people who were totally loyal to him. This had, of course, obvious psychological compensations and political benefits for him. However, such loyalty meant that there could be little distancing between himself and his aides, since loyalty in hierarchic structures degenerates into blind obedience. Those blindly obedient to political power and authority invariably display bad manners to those who are outside the circle of power. This has the effect of endangering the leader himself, who must then accept total responsibility for his coterie. But such a leader hardly ever does so since his primary interest is in survival. Thus, he continues to think of ways to sacrifice others in order to protect himself.

As late as the summer of 1973, immediately after the existence of the tapes was revealed to the Ervin Committee and the nation, Nixon could have stated that he intended to destroy them because they were his private tapes, his personal notes: his intended "gift" to the American people at the proper time. Imagine a bonfire on television, in which he destroyed the tapes. What could have been done? Who would have stopped it? What a terrifying lesson in executive power we would have received. Goldwater said he would have burned the tapes. Others will next time. (It is interesting that no congressman has proposed that as a matter of law future Presidents should be required to keep tapes of their conversations so that they can be used as evidence in a future impeachment crisis. Nor has Congress proposed this check against its own members.)

Nixon had not understood how deep the American crisis had gone and how frightened and lethargic the congressional institutions were. His belief that it was necessary to feign honesty while shouting that he played by the "rules" did not credit the exhaustion of the American people. Those who called for "full disclosure" throughout the Watergate episode were saying, in effect, that no moral standard exists in America except to admit forthrightly one's own corrupt activities. It was no longer necessary to be hypocritical, they were saying, it was enough to be sincere.

Sincerity is a minor human virtue, but at least it is a virtue. Nixon did not catch the clue. Had he understood that in the old System, vice timely admitted by power is sufficient to vindicate the powerful, he would have saved his reputation and that of his retinue.

The platitude that hypocrisy is the tax which vice pays to virtue applied to Nixon. The level of anger and disgust at Nixon rose as he appeared to be holding back not only information, but a degree of decisiveness that local and institutional leaderships expect of a commander-in-chief. As the months wore on, Nixon revealed more of his activities. Both the revelations and the form in which they were disclosed brought a new dimension to Watergate.* Commentary became more and more taken up with the search for "the real Nixon." Even he joined in the search. Was he a man, a President, an office, a role, a symbol? Was he more than a bundle of roles wearing the tattered cloak of legitimacy? It was a search that struck terror in the hearts of many men—those who had given themselves up to a corporate or managerial role that had no discernible human form. Many Americans secretly wondered whether they had all disappeared into a System which defied human dimension and meaning. Journalists often said of Nixon that when he was alone in a room there was no one present. Was this existentially true of the rest of us? Perhaps Nixon had kept the tapes of himself and his brethren not primarily for blackmail or a future tax deduction. Perhaps it was to reassure himself that he existed, *was there,* and had a true face. For people of

* Once the tapes were released Nixon's fellow Republicans saw the Watergate flooded with a new problem. Members of Congress and the Republican party recalled that virtue (virtuosity) had a moral dimension. For Nixon, this meant that while he might be able to continue in office, he would have lost not only his administration, but all chance of an honored place in children's history books. People wanted old verities or a new ethics. All politicians were now being held to some new definition of ethics that might replace those of the marketplace. But what those new ethics might be remained undefined.

Nixon's generation, the word "tape" has many connotations. It holds things together, guards the skin, and keeps out foreign bodies as the true or natural "face" mends or heals. Once this tape is lifted it reveals a true "face." For Nixon, however, the technological tapes revealed that he was a hypocrite, a poseur, even an imposter, who had no true face.

Members of Congress continued to call for Nixon's "unmasking," unwilling to believe that there was nothing beneath the mask. Nixon was merely a set of appearances, clichés, and more masks—like an actor who had long ago given up trying to fix a consistent identity. He could find himself only in the roles he was called upon to play. The truths and lies ran together for Nixon; and so he not only deceived others, but he deceived himself as well. Socrates has said: "Appear to yourself as you wish to appear to others." But the hypocrite does not know how to present himself to the world because he feels, in part, that he is not worthy. In the Quaker tradition, the spirit of public confession is an important one. It is here where the person is to come forward from the heart with what he feels and who he is. Those who cover up this feeling cover up conscience; they must forever see themselves as hypocrites. Hannah Arendt has pointed out:

> Psychologically speaking, one may say that the hypocrite is too ambitious; not only does he want to appear virtuous before others, he wants to convince himself. By the same token, he eliminates from the world, which he has populated with illusions and lying phantoms, the only core of integrity from which true appearance could arise again, his own incorruptible self. . . . As witnesses not of our intentions but of our conduct, we can be true or false and the hypocrite's crime is that he bears false witness against himself. What makes it so plausible to assume that hypocrisy is the vice of vices is that integrity can indeed exist under the cover of all other vices except this one. Only

crime and the criminal, it is true, confront us with the perplexity of radical evil; but only the hypocrite is rotten to the core.[1]

Nixon was beset by a series of personality and policy contradictions which dictated his public decline. It is possible to see the contradictions of the System itself in transition. Like other Presidents in a television-conscious age, his time was spent concentrating on how things appeared, not on what they were. Thus, he was supremely anxious about the media, always trying to find ways to discipline the owners of TV stations and newspapers so they in turn would discipline the journalists and reporters. He spoke as if he wanted to return power to the states, but his policies were an attempt to centralize control in the White House. Yet he did not know how to get control over the bureaucracy despite the fact that bureaucracies, by their nature, favor centralization. He spoke as if he were a "strict constructionist" in interpreting the Constitution, yet he insisted on the sanctity of national power as against the people, except where issues of property and the corporation were involved. He endeavored to present himself as a DAR patriot at a time when the flag of patriotism seemed to be shifting from the hands of the imperialists to those who had more modest appetites for the United States role in the world.

Nixon believed the time had come to restore proxy wars and a fulsome use of the CIA in place of American military engagement. Yet the CIA thought him a fumbler who did not "use" the agency efficiently, preferring to implant his junto over them. The result, they thought, would endanger their continuous and historic imperialist mission. He thought he could coopt the leaders of other nations into the American "Presidency," but he forgot that flattery of certain leaders breeds envy among others. Moreover, few leaders in the world, if any, are as free as an American President has been to commit singlehandedly the entire nation to a particular course. Nixon was a symbol manipulator who believed that politics had nothing to do with social program, hence nothing to do with people's lives. He feared such programs because they could stir up the poorer classes.

There were ideas and contradictions, devoid of either consistent ideology or coherent political content. Nixon believed that politics as it related to public action had to do with symbol manipulation and appearances, rather than the representation of people's needs. Thus, he did not translate his policies into an effective program that would have enabled his new elite to accomplish anything more than the shift of *appearances* of power to themselves. They would have to leave the actual power firmly rooted in the established economic, political and social elites of the old System: the finance bankers of Wall Street, the Council on Foreign Relations, the industrial capitalists such as Ford, the network media, the banks, the insurance empires, and the multinational corporations which flew only the flag of profit.

Without a consistent series of policies or a consciousness of themselves as a "new class" (because they were not a new class), Nixon and his group remained a clique which, on a daily basis, had to continue to do the bidding of established power if they were to maintain any semblance of running the government. Nixon's group was unable to develop a "modern," nonhypocritical philosophy of government which would have exempted Nixon's friends from hardship or punishment while simultaneously subjecting others to control. Thus, privilege (private law, exemption) and prerogative (principles taken for granted when used by a more established ruling group) were immediately questioned when used by Nixon. Once he faltered, Nixon became again nothing but the gritty Okie, the gut fighter who remained an outsider and who could not develop a "new American majority" or a national consciousness which put the established forces in their place. His self-sufficiency principles, his idea that it was the individual against the state—and against other individuals—destroyed his political successes.

Thus, Nixon's mistake was not that he wanted martial law in America as well as the perpetuation of imperial proxy wars in Southeast Asia (policies to which the traditional elites did not overly object, but even supported); it was not that he had attempted to set up an internal police state mechanism whose purpose was the transformation of law into order. Nor was Nixon's demise due to diplomatic inflexibility; after all, he had developed a policy of détente in the context of imperial spheres of influence. He protected the various corporate groups such as ITT, soft-drink companies like Pepsico, and oil companies—all searching for new markets and cheap labor costs abroad, efforts which would be jointly protected by the United States and the "host" country—socialist, capitalist, or otherwise.

Nixon's other mistakes clustered around his inability to obtain either obedience or compromise with the domestic bureaucracy. While aversion to bureaucracy is a popular position in American politics, politicians too often discount its economic and political importance. One out of every seven Americans works for the State either in its federal, state, or local manifestations. By rejecting or ignoring this material reality, by not accepting the bureaucracy's own reason for existence (or developing one for them), Nixon was not able to get control over the government itself, or do the things that became a matter of daily business for those who accept the importance of bureaucracy. His problem was not knowing how to perform a purge of government officials who had come to like the power and status of their jobs without endangering his own position and that of his retinue. Lower-level bureaucrats in the CIA and FBI felt threatened by Nixon's group. And they put great pressure on their own "barons" to defend them and their work. (As a general rule, purges of governments in modern times are most effective where there is no free press. Where a free press does exist, there is the possibility of trouble for the leader.)

As more information leaked out, Nixon's enemies learned that his retinue had no collective ideology which would sustain them. The processors had very little loyalty to one another once they were stripped of state power and the President's paternal hand was withdrawn from their shoulders. Without ideology and group loyalty Nixon's men were reduced to a band of hapless, lonely individuals. A leader's task is to find ways that his retinue can have loyalty outside of role to each other which is predicated on ideology of purpose and interest. If loyalty extends only to him, they all court personal disaster.

Nixon's most significant error was in his failure to understand correctly how he could use the state bureaucracy in relation to the corporations and unions. The 1972 election showed that Nixon could have secured the help and support of the corporations, the unions, the "public interest" groups and the universities in developing a "rationing" system to follow after his own Phase II attempts at economic controls. Democratic party leaders would have supported this as a move toward price and wage control— which they had publicly insisted on. Nixon, for example, refused to ration fuel products at a time when he could have used the fuel "shortage" to strengthen his political position.

Nixon seemed to believe sincerely that rationing and controls would destroy capitalism. He failed to realize that the System itself operates in the private sector on the basis of administered prices which are set by and between the managers of different corporations and the managers of labor unions. In other words, prices and wages, as well as rationing, would have continued to operate the same way they did "privately"—with the same groups setting prices and wages, but now legitimated by state power. To the media and the American audience, Nixon would thus have given the appearance of a President acting in the public interest.

In other words, Nixon foundered on his reluctance to interfere with capitalism at a time when capitalism could have been helped by state power even more than it presently is. The major corporations knew that the bureaucracies, far from disciplining them, in fact "greased the skids" for the largest 1,000 corporations. He could have successfully thwarted his detractors by appearing to work for the harassed and economically declining middle and working classes, by managing the economy through rationing and wage/price boards and a new monitoring system of economic police which would operate like the old draft board system in each American precinct. He could thus have not only rebuilt the bureaucracy into his own tool, but also added to it profoundly greater police power, more than he was able to obtain in the 1970–72 period when he used the radicals as a pretext for increasing the size of the "peace" forces in the United States.

Only if he had carried out the wishes of those who insisted on state controls over the economy would Nixon have been able to save his reputation: citizens would willingly have become not only the instruments but the supporters of his definition of state power. No one would have seriously challenged him had he used the formula of stewardship that Roosevelt II had used, the formula blessed by Henry Stimson and members of all the established ruling groups. He would have created the appearance of intervention on behalf of the people, when in fact, such intervention would have continued to serve only the interests of the most powerful and highly organized economic groups.

For those who are corrupt and whose corruption is discovered, their best personal protection is to reach out for greater areas of power, thus giving up any notions about limited power of the state. They must then attempt to make their corruption into a legal principle. The supreme political irony of the economic crisis since 1971 is that if the President had adopted the suggestions of Senator Henry Jackson or Congresswoman Bella Abzug for controls over the economy—which would have meant, in practice, exercising control with the cooperation and support (cooption) of leaderships of the largest organization economic units—he might have escaped unscathed from Watergate.

5 / The Impeached System

The congressional attempt to take back power from the Executive resulted in a number of surprises. It became clear that members of Congress, when not sufficiently coopted into the President's ratifying process, could be irritating and querulous, disturbing the tranquility of the country. Congress could encourage public discussion and even entrap itself into acting beyond personal privilege to an assumption of constitutional responsibilities. Congress had put itself on record against undeclared wars. This might mean that if an appropriate occasion presented itself, an enraged Congress might even press for impeachment under certain circumstances. The impeachment proceedings, and the long-term political effect of such an atmosphere, meant that the President would have to calculate whether a rambunctious Congress kept some club in its cloakroom which it could use against him. In late 1973, the club seemed to be a small one. Nixon did not believe that Congress would assert its power either *against* imperialism or *for* significant change in the operating procedures that his outfit had fashioned during the latter part of his first term. He believed, as did Jefferson, that the constitutional weapon of impeachment was a "scarecrow."

No one who believed in the System wanted to reduce the Presidency, a term which seemed to describe a fourth branch of government. Nor was there interest in bringing about the social changes that would have been the prod and the result of impeachment. In Nixon's view, Congress was another audience, a body to be informed and, if necessary, reluctantly stroked. It was not, however, to be considered as an independent source of will with a direction of its own. Its members might intimidate bureaucrats, as he and Joe McCarthy had done a generation before, but it could not change the direction that a willful President intended to take.

Nixon and his generation had grown up in a period when Presidents could say anything, believing that a mass audience would supinely applaud. It was not likely that Congress and the people would pierce the presidential façade of superior, disinterested knowledge and authority. Nixon had learned this as a freshman senator. He had seen how President Truman took the country into the Korean war on his own initiative and then had stated, in a presidential proclamation, that a national emergency existed which required that "any and all threats against our national security" be repelled and "that the full moral and material strength of the Nation may be readied for the dangers which threaten us." [1]

It was Nixon's self-destructive manner and his inability to coopt the established leaderships which caused the issue of impeachment to be raised seriously by Congress. Amid the seemingly endless waves of accusation, indictment, and allegations against the processors and Nixon, attempts were made by some constitutionalists to formulate a structural and political rationale for impeachment. It was generally perceived that men of power should maintain standards and be held accountable for their acts. But which acts? And how? The impeachment process went beyond the particular case of Nixon since it could, potentially, restore a crude balance of power between the President and Congress. It was thought that the President and the citizenry would learn that Congress had a trump card and the will to play it.

Nixon assumed that such a card would never be played. In the winter of 1972, when Nixon developed his law-and-order position—but exempted the state from such strictures—Attorney General Richard Kleindienst taunted a congressional committee by saying that the President could withhold any document from the Congress and stop any government official from testifying on the grounds of executive privilege. When questioned by members of Congress about the sweeping nature of this position, devoid of legal precedent, Kleindienst told them that if they did not like the President's position, they had a constitutional right to impeach him.

After the extent of corruption, bribery, deceit, and fraud had been detailed by Congress, the press, and a newly purged Justice Department, the President's lawyer argued in the courts that the President could not be ordered to give over the tapes of White House conversations. If the Congress was so exercised about presidential behavior, its proper recourse was impeachment. Nixon's lawyers, in the arguments they used before the courts, insisted that impeachment proceedings—and not indictment—were the only recourse against a President for criminal acts. His lawyers said in court that the President was "immune, unless and until he has been impeached, from the sanctions of the criminal law, impeachment is the device that ensures that he is not above justice, and trial of impeachment is left to the Senate and not to the courts." [2] The political judgment of the White House was that Congress was pusillanimous and would not act to impeach. However, when the House Judiciary Committee began its determination of the impeachment standards to be applied, the President's new counsels adopted the standard that a President could not be impeached except for criminally indictable offenses. But how was this to be determined? Were his crimes against the System? Against the Constitution? Against the people?

Until Congress successfully overrode Nixon's veto of the War Powers bill, Congress had been unable to marshal enough votes to override any of his vetoes, even of those programs which had popular support. Within a two-month period of testing between the White House and Congress, Nixon's opponents failed seven times to override his veto. Once Nixon was overridden on the War Powers bill, and Republican congressmen continued their voluntary retirement from Congress, an impeachment inquiry resolution was drawn and adopted by the House. The unintended effect of the impeachment resolution seemed to be that of cutting the Presidency to manageable proportions. The areas outlined by the Judiciary Committee implied that a President could be impeached, and possibly convicted, for actions which were anathema to the general purposes of the Constitution and repugnant to the standards expected of government officials. The events and acts detailed in the Watergate revelations—including acts of war which some considered criminal—stirred a timid attempt to assert the accountability of government officials. In a related context, a former justice of the Supreme Court, Tom Clark, said that "the one who is called upon to enforce the orders of the President would look to the Constitution and be guided by it. Otherwise, he would suffer the penalties of Nuremburg." [3]

The categories chosen by the Judiciary Committee for its impeachment investigation—bribery, coverup, dirty tricks, impoundment, favors to corporations, waging secret war in Southeast Asia, tax evasion, the Huston Plan—amounted to a condemnation not only of a President, but also of imperialism, presidential power, and capitalism: the System itself. Impeachment and conviction might open up the entire System to radical surgery. John Dean, in his testimony before the Senate Watergate Committee, said that he had warned Nixon that "there was a cancer growing on the Presidency." Indeed, some had begun to sense the malignancy was not confined to the body of the President or the "Presidency"—but was symptomatic of the entire political and economic System. Congressmen were frightened by such implications and the result was an attempt to narrow the complaints against Nixon. The secret war in Southeast Asia was viewed as "high policy" rather than crime, and impoundment was seen as a "policy alternative" which a President could pursue as a solemn act of statecraft.

Along with generations of American schoolchildren, politicians had been taught that it was a terrible "mistake" to have impeached Andrew Johnson. In our own time, John Kennedy, in *Profiles in Courage*, was full of praise for the "courageous" senator who saved Andrew Johnson from being convicted in the Senate.[1] But most Americans did not know the facts about the impeachment of Andrew Johnson which suggested a very different interpretation. The mistake was not that he was impeached. It was that he was not convicted.

After the Civil War, the radical Republicans wanted Reconstruction policy to include land reform and a civil rights act which would enforce the new constitutional amendments. Neither was acceptable to Andrew Johnson who refused to enforce the laws of Congress which guaranteed civil rights to blacks. He rejected the generally held view of the Republican party that the "South should not be reinstated into the Union until there were adequate guarantees that the slaves liberated by the nation should enjoy the rights of free men." [5]

Congressional leaders were furious at Johnson for not supporting their civil rights position. Their fury stemmed from two important roots. One was the question of the power relationship between the President and Congress. It was only seventy-five years since the first Congress. Hence, both houses were still full of their own preeminence as against the Presidency. The United States could speak only if Congress spoke. It was not, in their view, the President who spoke for the United States. On the eve of the Civil War in 1860, Congress vigorously asserted this position against the hapless James Buchanan. President Buchanan had informed the Congress that the President "is the direct representative on earth of the people of all and each of the sovereign states. To them, and to them alone is he responsible while acting within the sphere of his constitutional duty, and not in any manner to the House of Representatives." [6] The congressional response, although now buried in the dusty precedents of the Congress, was ferocious:

> *Resolved,* That the House dissents from the doctrines of the special message of the President of the United States of March 28, 1860;
>
> That the extent of power contemplated in the adoption of the resolutions of inquiry of March 5, 1860, is necessary to the proper discharge of the constitutional duties devolved upon Congress;
>
> That judicial determinations, the opinions of former Presidents, and uniform usage sanction its exercise; and,
>
> That to abandon it would leave the executive department of the Government without supervision or responsibi-

NOTES ON THE OLD SYSTEM

lity, and would be likely to lead to a concentration of power in the hands of the President, dangerous to the rights of a free people.

The committee contended that

The President of the United States, under the Constitution, possesses neither privilege nor immunity beyond the humblest citizen, and is less favored in this respect than Senators and Representatives in Congress. Article I, section 6, reads: "They [the Senators and Representatives] shall, in all cases except treason, felony, and breach of the peace, be privileged from arrest during their attendance at the session of their respective Houses, and in going to and returning from the same." No such exemption is made in behalf of the Executive or any other officer of Government. The conduct of the President is always subject to the constitutional supervision and judgment of Congress; while he, on the contrary, has no such power over either branch of that body. He is left, under the law, without shield or protection of any kind, except such as is borne by all. He is as amenable for all his acts after inauguration as before. He can make no plea which is denied to any other citizen, and is subject to the same scrutiny, trial, and punishment, with the proceedings, hazards, and penalties of impeachment superadded. The President and the citizen stand upon equality of rights. The distinction between them arises from an inequality of duties. Wherever the conduct of the latter is open to inquiry and charge, that of the former is not the less so. The President affirms, with seeming seriousness, in comparing himself with the House of Representatives, that, "as a coordinate branch of the Government, he is their equal." This is denied in emphatic terms. He is "coordinate," but not coequal. He is "coordinate," for he "holds the same rank;" but he is not coequal, for his immunities and powers are less. The Members of the House may claim a privilege, whether right or wrong, which he can not, and the executive or law-executing power must always be inferior to the legislative or law-making power. The latter is omnipotent within the limits of the Constitution; the former is subject not only to the Constitution, but to the determinations of the latter also. To repeat the point: *The President is not, in any respect, superior to the citizen, merely because he is bound to discharge more numerous duties; and he is not coequal with that branch of Government which helps to impose and define those duties.*[7] [Emphasis added.]

After the Civil War, the legal and constitutional question of which govermental branch was preeminent came down to which branch controlled the army. Reciprocally, the question was, Which policies would the leadership of the army favor? Congress passed an Army Appropriations Act which stated that all military orders of the Executive should be issued through the secretary of war.[8] He was not to be removed, or assigned to other duties, without the consent of the Senate. When Andrew Johnson removed Secretary of War Edwin Stanton, replacing him with Major General Lorenzo Thomas, Johnson intended to get rid of a man who was friendly to those favoring strong civil rights legislation and who would enforce the legislation through the army. Stanton's firing meant that the army's policies would now favor Johnson's posture on civil rights.

Johnson had another purpose as well: the castration of Congress's constitutional power to regulate the use of the armed forces of the United States. This became the second underlying cause of the impeachment. Johnson remained in the Presidency after impeachment, having received the support of General Ulysses Grant, an Eisenhower-like figure of the time. Johnson's political survival had far-reaching and ominous consequences for the political economy of the country and its social system: it engendered the acceptance by the Republican business class of the southern aristocracy's continued control over the land ownership and allowed the perpetuation of slavery by establishing the social system within the framework of the Constitution—while constitutional rights for blacks went unenforced. The result was a sixty-five-year period of American feudalism without obligations and a capitalism without dignity or equal opportunity.

The effect on Congress was striking and instructive. Congress gradually lost regulatory power over the armed forces. In the twentieth century, influence exercised by Congress over the armed forces was mediated through the southern bourbons and committee chairmen who believed that the growth of the armed forces, the imperial growth of the United States as a nation, is the only politically acceptable way to develop the South. Military bases, defense installations, and defense factories have been the federal mechanism for ensuring southern white "prosperity."

In Nixon's time, few radicals or liberals had developed a consistent or coherent program that would enable either them or their ideas to struggle for center stage. While occasionally there was dim recognition that impeachment, as a constitutional procedure, might open the way for profound changes, there was confusion about whether impeachment was a cause or an effect of those changes. The debates in Congress were devoid of discussion about program, and the members of Congress seemed equally devoid of ambition or ideas. Some, it is true, believed that impeachment was intended as a national inquest, a means to develop a national program. It was a way to resolve the crucial egalitarian issues raised by the American Civil War—within the framework shaped by Martin Luther King, Jr., and the civil rights and antiwar movements. But labor unions, consumer groups, and remnants of the antiwar movement were unable to join together either for Nixon's impeachment or for a common program. The

Democratic party's leadership insisted that no issues be raised that would affect the narrow question of Richard Nixon's impeachment. Congressmen insisted that the issues of impeachment were *not* political and did not involve questions of program. A studied attempt was made to "neutralize" the impeachment proceedings, thereby further insulating not only its object, the Presidency, but also the Congress, from the people. The citizenry remained a sometimes fascinated, sometimes bored audience.

Nixon believed he knew the underlying issues that would decide the outcome of impeachment. Early in 1974, he called various members of Congress to his office. In the course of his conversation, he pointed to his telephone and said that his power was awesome. He could pick up "that phone," he said, and "order the death of 70 million people."

Who would or could control the military and nuclear weapons during an impeachment proceeding? To whom would the military owe its allegiance? What would our major "adversaries" and "friends" in the world say at a time when there was international instability and inflation across the entire American imperium? Was there a social and political program that Congress could rally around and project to the country after an impeachment? Would there be a greater flight of capital from the United States through the multinational corporations, further diminishing the allegiance of the American economic oligarchs to the United States and further depressing the internal economic development of the American society? Would a leaderless government, plus a runaway inflation, set the ground for "revolution"? Was it perhaps better to have a President who had isolated himself than one who would strengthen the military further, defeating the economic détente? Was it enough for Congress to brandish its club but never to use it? The media concentrated on other questions, and as far as the public knew, the entire issue of impeachment was a legalistic one having no political content or consequences. The truth, however, was otherwise.

The tragic political puzzle for the country with regard to impeachment was that the assumptions and methods of imperialism had been lovingly formed by *both* major parties, although they differed over the mode of achieving imperial control at home and abroad. The two-party system had closed people to both policy and systemic alternatives. The country heard only the voices of the confused Democratic party. Hubert Humphrey's views about national security were, in fact, not so different from those of Nixon—nor, for that matter, were his coterie's fund raising tactics. Senator Stuart Symington from Missouri, who was an architect of the national security state, continued to defend the CIA. He managed William Colby's appointment as CIA director even though Colby had served as chief of the pacification program in Vietnam (Operation Phoenix) and was a man who, in other circumstances, might have stood in the dock condemned as a war criminal.[9]

Moreover, while leaders of American corporations, nominal Democrats, appeared on Nixon's Enemy List, their real concern was whether their overseas markets would be bombed by enraged mobs. Their fear with regard to Nixon's policies was economic, not political. For them, *the* question remained: Could Nixon manage the empire? That Nixon had cooled street opposition at home and disengaged from the war without losing the economic sphere of influence in Southeast Asia suggested to the corporate heads that Nixon was not a bad manager. Furthermore, what were the alternatives? They were hardly revolutionaries who intended to challenge or change the American system of imperialism. Indeed, Nixon had opened up new markets for them in China and the Soviet Union. And of course they were no more in favor of land reform or equal rights than the bourbons who gained from the impeachment defeat of the radical reconstructionists in Andrew Johnson's time. There was, however, an important contradiction embedded in all this.

The White House horrors, as John Mitchell called them, exposed the American governing process for all to see. To forestall a politically revolutionary consciousness, it was necessary to develop a theory that Nixon and his activities were distinguishable from the System's usual operations. In other words, Nixon had to be perceived by a majority in Congress and the media, as well as by the American audience, as a pathological occupant of the Presidency. If the citizenry at large began to see Nixon as a logical successor and legitimate (legal) heir to the Presidencies of Jefferson, Lincoln, Wilson, the Roosevelts, Truman, Kennedy, and Johnson, then the habit of obedience in the middle and working classes might be broken—and the ruling elites in the institutions and corporations might themselves be undone. The ironist would say that the System was "working." But it was not working for the common good.

If people decided that Nixon as a President was no different from others, it could result in greater instability and a possible internal upheaval against the elites who exercised broad control over the society through various interconnecting links in banking, insurance, transportation, oil, and steel. The oligarchs of these institutions would be poisoned because the audience might come to see that the Nixon clique and the oligarchs all drank at the same well. The officials of the government, whose task since the Second World War involved murder, bribery, etc., had to differentiate themselves from Nixon. Thus, valiant efforts were made by the CIA, military, and police bureaucracies to distinguish Nixon and his operations from the way the System usually operated. Efforts were made to distinguish between bribing foreign officials and bribing American officials, fixing elections abroad and fixing

them within the United States, assassinating foreigners and assassinating Americans, spying on the Left as against spying on
established figures in the Democratic party. It was crucial for
maintaining the loyalty of large numbers of Americans to make
such distinctions about policies and events. The heads of large
bureaucracies and corporations used the opportunity to recapture
their autonomy so that a President would be hampered if, in the
future, he tried to reach within their organization to assert direction over them.

Watergate dispelled the myth that politics could stop at the
water's edge. It was clear that to administer an empire, the methods
used abroad were ones that would be used within the United
States. Nixon was the necessary next stage in the administration of
the national security state and the American imperium. There was
a correlative fear expressed by some members of Congress who
were not wholly wound up in their physical exercises in the House
and Senate gym. This fear was that the newly revealed methods of
elite statecraft—bribery, threat, violence, intimidation—might become instruments of the poor and the middle class who would
employ them against the elites and even against one another. Thus,
the society would become quite unlivable and ultimately would
dissolve into a Hobbesian state of nature. Some indication of this
potential was seen in groups of the oppressed and frustrated who
formed themselves into kidnapping gangs for both political and
"macho" purposes. In San Francisco there was random terror in
the streets as well as carefully planned assassinations and kidnap-
pings. In the East and Middle West, members of the working class
who were self-employed (the independent truckers) began a dis-
ruptive strike, shooting at members of the organized working class
(the Teamsters). Evening television showed films of truck convoys
guarded by police and national guardsmen with air cover. The
fervor which the social movements of the 1960s displayed in civil

rights and antiwar fused into traditional questions of class divisions and inequities.

Indeed, the objective conditions seemed volatile. While the poor and working class found themselves squeezed between inflation, recession, and shortages, the profits of the top 500 corporations were at an all-time high. It seemed obvious that the very definition of citizenship needed remolding since there was no longer any way that a reasonable person could believe that a Rockefeller and a Mississippi tenant farmer were citizens in the same nation. There was an unspoken sense of futility and cynicism in people about the meaning of citizenship—a citizen's rights were meaningless if a President was able to pay less income tax than a steelworker, able to send hundreds of thousands of troops to war on his own command, or press the button to rain nuclear weapons on anyone, solely on the basis of his own or a ruling elite's view of national interest. Nixon had been the beneficiary of these contradictions in the American System; he was also caught and trapped by them. But so, it seemed, was everyone else.

6 / Law and the State

I have discussed Nixon as a political character in some detail because he reflects a character type which emerges from the struggle that is now raging within the government and the body politic itself. Richard Nixon is not a pathological exception to American life. He combines within himself the turbulence and the contradictions of the successful man in America. He appears to us as featureless. At first he seems to be the classic political broker who acts for old ruling-class interests while hating the airs of those who manifest such interests and pretensions. But by the end of his first term, we see him as a man who hoped to consolidate his power with his own junto. He intended to make the barons of the corporations pay tribute to his new group. We see him wearing many masks and behaving less like a man than a bundle of roles. He is a synthetic national personality who has grown within our midst to rule our lives and dominate other nations.

In twentieth-century America, the synthetic personality has

been characteristic of politicians, even those with greater depth to their character. Lyndon Johnson once wrote an article in the *Texas Quarterly* describing his synthesis and credo. He was an American, a father, a farmer, a Democrat, a capitalist, a worker, etc.[1] When a politician presents himself in this way, he is saying that constituencies do not have to organize for their own objectives because they can count on the leader-broker to comprehend their needs; he is part of them, but always a bit more. Brokering one group to another within the limits of capitalism and imperialism has become the norm for the modern American politician. Therefore, we cannot understand Nixon's political character without understanding the profound struggles of the System which the Indochina war heightened and brought into the open. It was the Indochinese who braked the engine of American imperialism abroad. At home the mutually reinforcing dynamic between stated American ideals and the attempts of blacks, women, and other excluded groups to realize them generated a new sense of politics and opened the possibility of an affirmative transformation of the American state.

From what I have suggested in the earlier Notes, certain conclusions can be drawn. One is that the American System, by its nature and its development, is jerry-built. It never quite resolves fundamental problems. It merely engulfs them in new ones, attempting to contain within itself massive antagonistic contradictions, masking them through the pleasing language of problem solving, coordination, and efficiency. The ruling elites have no agreed upon long-term conception of their own interests, let alone anyone else's, and the huge bureaucracy based on hierarchy reflects its own internal dynamics in its middle levels.*

---

* While bureaucrats adapt to the status system of the society generally, with their families tied to the values of the consumer culture, the bureaucracy emphasizes its own values, privileges, and career patterns in the middle and upper reaches. Bureaucrats live insulated and protected lives. Their families are not as vulnerable to economic insecurity as others are within the society.

We can divide the modern evolution of the American state into three stages. It should be understood, however, that each overlaps the other, causing contradictions and splits between various political actors and institutional groupings. A new stage of political transformation does not begin in antagonism to the prior stage. Men who are already powerful actors in one stage will invariably seek to preserve dominant aspects of that period even if they support massive changes.

The first stage was founded on class law which protected the growth of corporate capitalism and its expansion. No burdens or restrictions were to be placed on the free movement of commerce throughout the nation and then the world. The corporation itself was understood to be the most rational means of gathering profits, organizing work and, of course, limiting liability. The state was the night watchman for the society and the bodyguard for business. The expansion of capitalism meant taking in the bodyguard as a partner. Thus, businessmen acceded to some intervention in the economy. The military and national security state bureaucracy sustained a worldwide imperium which entailed the transformation of corporate capitalism itself. The new stage (Stage II) was characterized by high levels of military spending; a system of expensive military alliances resulting in continuous military engagement; bureaucratic intervention into industries through government contracts; and synthetic law grounded in hierarchy, secrecy, and obedience. This process led to the sharing of baronial power with the bureaucracy, its policy makers, and the military. The third stage emerged when Nixon's group attempted to take control of the state apparatus with management ideas that reflected principles of militarism, internal policing and monopoly power. To save the national security state governing mode and its assumption that the United States was "Number 1," Nixon and his group "ended" the war with Indochina and sought to silence the mob. To do so meant that they had to change the very nature of the National Security State. The major transition was from a bureaucracy that initiated activities along fairly well defined internal rules of behavior to one that carried out activities initiated and directed by the leader. John Ehrlichman explained this point of view when he said,

> We don't want or need ideas from out there [the bureaucracy and the people]. That's the sort of thing we're trying to get away from. Ideas breed programs and programs breed bureaucracy. *We get all the ideas we need from the President.* And our job is just to execute.[2]

The transition within the national security area had begun with Kennedy who hoped to gain control over the bureaucracy and make it into his instrument early in 1961. The crisis deepened with Johnson, although it was masked because of the emormous increase in the bureaucracy.

I will now elaborate to some degree on each of these stages. My hope is that further inquiry into them will provide a clue into what future political action should be taken by the citizenry.

Stage I: Class Law and Corporate Capitalism

We may note certain characteristics of class law within the United States. This term does not include all common law. It does, however, refer to the development of modern corporate rules of property and commerce. Politically, class law is the judicial and legislative means used by the most powerful people and commercial interests in the society to ensure protection of their property and personal lives. It is the legitimizing instrument of the entrepreneur and the large corporations. Class law attempts to protect, therefore, large private economic interests and seeks to limit state power over them. Its most profound early statements can be found in Supreme Court cases after 1877 which immunized corporations under the Fourteenth Amendment as if they were people.[3] From 1877 to at least 1954 the Fourteenth Amendment served the corporations, not black people. Class law is public in that it is applied by the courts and is publicly discussed and enunciated by the large property holders of the society. The public debate is usually limited to lawyers, judges, and investors. The rules they fashion are meant to guarantee calculability, stability, the control of future events, and continuous access to productive resources, whether human or natural. Their concern is that each area be seen as a market to sell and a place to buy. No community was to develop or apply burdens limiting the sale of goods or the extraction of materials.

From time to time, poorer elements in the society may benefit from class law—as when a poor person sets himself up as a corporation to limit his debt liability, or when a small businessman receives damages from a corporate giant as a result of unfair competitive practices, or when a shopkeeper can prevent clerks from organizing in the shop. But when such benefits occur, they are generally the result of accident rather than design.

Until Theodore Roosevelt, class law required that the state not interfere in the property arrangements of the corporation or the market. But the definition of property changed, and the role of the state, if it were to protect property, changed as well.

> ... the modern concept of property has evolved from the holding of things to the control of the supply of things through the transactions of persons, so that it signifies the four personal relations of buyer and seller, creditor and debtor, competitors, and governors and governed.[4]

The state found itself having a positive duty to interfere in the market mechanism, if for no other reason than that capitalists found themselves on all sides of these transactions and looked for help wherever they could get it. Interference by those who wielded state power, however, was to be through the courts and regulatory commissions which would set the framework for operations of the government and the corporations. Once capitalism continued in its "peaceful expansion," transforming itself into monopoly capitalism, it required a different form of class law. The state became an active participant. Administrative procedures and regulations stemming from general laws written by Congress or state assemblies talked about the "public interest." This meant that the state would "guarantee the future" by setting quotas, subsidies, and rationalizing competition within industry and commerce through regulatory commissions. Economics was to be the domain of the administrator and Executive rather than the Legislative. Social reformers in the universities argued for an administrative system of economics that would transcend the marketplace and the politics of the legislatures or courts. The "best" thinking in the universities argued that issues should be taken out of the forums of Congress and local town halls. These forums were to be replaced by the dispassionate hand of the administrator in the public or private bureaucracy. Their terms of art were "efficiency," "productivity," "growth," and "management." Such terms fitted perfectly with monopoly expansion.

It was not until Roosevelt II that class law took on changed meanings as the state was called upon to stabilize the economy on a daily basis. New regulations in banking, crop production, mining, transportation, securities, housing, and labor relations meant that the state apparatus was to be heavily involved in defining the economy.

In practice, laws and regulations have emerged from "lobbying" or drafting activities by lawyers and their corporate clients. Laws as they came to be written were little more than a series of generalized statements, the meaning of which could only become clear through their administration and enforcement. (Antitrust law, for example, was inhibitive rather than proscriptive.) The executive bureaucracy determined the *meaning* of the laws, often relying for actual drafts on the private ruling group most directly affected. (On the other hand, some laws were passed in Congress which had astounding specificity, being clearly designed to benefit one particular corporation or a few individuals. The legislation to save Lockheed or the Pennsylvania Railroad are examples. From time to time, one can note similar situations in the tax laws which are publicly arrived at but whose benefits are applicable only to a few. Such laws may be termed "bills of attainder *for* the few.")

Leadership elites expected the President to act as the national steward. And the President became the point man for this new mode of economic rationalization. Yet the President's power to act in this way did not come from the economics of capitalism. The roots were older. Presidential prerogatives stemmed from prerogatives of a king, who, it was thought, protected the realm through whatever means he thought necessary. In American politics the President bestowed upon himself the power of dealing with emergencies, crises, and difficult situations according to his view of the national interest. (As I have said, Locke assumed that the king's view of interest might not be the same as that of the "people" and therefore the right of revolution by the property holders remained intact.)

The use of class law as a way of imposing corporate command decisions by the managers and the owning groups has come under severe attack, and law itself has begun to take into account the demands of consumers and workers. Regulatory commissions operated as a shield for the corporation against a passive public which thought commissions were its agents. People found their own voices as the types of decisions made by the commissions stripped them of rights they thought were their own. Groups formed to express their own points of view at regulatory commission meetings which until the last decade were little more than honeymoon arrangements between the industry regulated and the most powerful elements in that industry.

There were certain other changes. Bureaucracies drafted regulations and Congress passed laws which covered entire sections of the population. It was not contemplated that the entire membership should apply for benefits. Bureaucracies and their clients concerned themselves with laws that were drafted in general terms and intended only for the few. However, the atmosphere of the 1960s caused people either to demand rights or avail themselves of rights that they supposedly had been granted. The most striking example was in welfare law, class law for the poor. Frances Piven and Richard Cloward recommended that welfare recipients organize to obtain their economic "benefits" by asserting rights ostensibly guaranteed to them.[5] Thus hundreds of thousands of people joined the welfare rolls. This legal strategy had as its objective fostering the redistribution of taxable income to the poor rather than the rich.

Nevertheless, the basic functions of class law were maintained. The largest corporations expanded, their markets were protected, state power was increasingly used in such a way as to formulate administrative regulations so that it favored the largest corporations. Bureaucrats enjoyed this new stage since it gave them larger domains to consider and shape. The group of client-states known as the "free world" became the opportunity for American bureaucrats to test out their pet ideas in the context of pressing forward American corporate, military, and cultural products.

Corporations that expanded abroad were given special advantages in the tax code and assistance from the CIA and military missions. The goals of the individual corporations, however, were not the same as those of the state bureaucracy. The corporations did not want to be bound by any state restrictions, whereas the bureaucrats' major activity is defining and enforcing restrictions, once benefits are granted and rules are fashioned. Such restrictions are usually applied against the weaker corporations in an arms' length way. There is a separate rule for the largest corporate units.

Stage II: Para-Law and the National Security State

Various strains within American political and economic history came together at the beginning of the Second World War. The United States gave up its status in 1940 as one of several great powers of the world to reach for the brass ring: world hegemony. The result was the development of a new kind of civil and military official who believed that the goal of American life was to maintain empire.

The post-World War II period was a time in which Rockefellers, Robert Lovett, John McCloy, and Averell Harriman were called public servants rather than capitalists protecting their interests. These men, it was supposed, had a broad perspective and were relieved of selfish motives or class interests. It was believed that all Americans had the same class interests and purposes as these men. These men were prepared to engage in continuous war, or split-second international atomic war, local brushfire involvement—in other words any military activity that would maintain the bureaucratic, military, and corporate delineation of the status quo. The people were exhorted to believe that what was good for capitalism, imperialism, and militarism was both good for the United States and necessary for their well-being.

Presidential emergency powers, legitimated in the war and

depression, could be used by officials and barons to stabilize the internal situation within the United States; and the same powers could be used as an instrument to court world hegemony. These forces were rationalized after the Second World War in a new stage of American political life, the national security state—a group of departments and autonomous agencies concerned with defense and warmaking, internal security, intelligence, as well as the massive sale of goods, services, and subsidies to and from the state.

A new form of law emerged in this period which has ersatz qualities. I have called it *para-law* because it is written in legal language although in the first instance it does not emerge from either legal decision, public debate, or congressional decision. It may happen however, that the courts and the legislative, because of their political weakness, will legitimate para-law after it is in effect. As a general rule para-law is forged in private outside the public forum, without public debate although it is made by public officials or executive proclamation. Since 1946 it has been created in bureaucracies, the military, and the executive to control and rationalize the activities of government so that they have some color of law attached to them. Para-law starts from the principle of hierarchy and institutionalized command. To a great extent para-law derives from judicially untested writ. Although it is not usually thought of as important, para-law governs the daily activities of millions of people who without the color of some form of custom and justification would be forced to see their work as criminal or merely an assertion of leadership power that has no limits within itself. Para-law attempts to develop limits and justifications through bureaucratic custom, intention, proclamation, and internal regulations that are derived from authority and hierarchy. Its primary legitimacy derives from power. In this sense it is the reverse of law in which power is to derive from law rather than law finding its roots only in power. Para-law has been crucial in sustaining the national security state, although Robert Borosage points out that para-law can be found in Roosevelt II's decrees on the economy prior to 1940.[6]

The national security state was the synthesis of state power and capitalism. Its emergence was a crucial step to keep a level of unity within the United States while sustaining an imperial or hegemonic thrust in the world. It was a way to straddle the line between fascism and socialism, the major state ideologies of the twentieth century. There was an inherent contradiction in the national security state. It was that continuous preparation for war, the distortion of the economy, the development of capitalists whose livelihood depends on the arms race and continuous covert and military engagement would not be contained as a self-enclosed bureaucratic process. It caused war abroad and mini-rebellions at home. War itself is of course a profoundly destabilizing dynamic which exacerbates all elements of the society, especially where the war is fought for "limited" or non-translatable purposes. It turned out that the national security state was a nondynamic system which could not afford continuous military expansion or military excitement—in other words, war. It could not afford arms budgets which would undermine business control over the internal economy. And it could not generate public support beyond ruling elites if it were engaged in anything but management of the empire.

This was the lesson that the Korean war taught various American leaders. But John Kennedy and the Democratic party did not believe the lesson of Korea. They toppled Eisenhower's military doctrine of limited military budgets and non-overt participation in war. The result was profound perturbations in the national security state. Once the United States sent ground forces to Indochina, the national security apparatus had to make great demands on a reluctant citizenry. The recalcitrant people attacked the national security apparatus and a vocal antiwar movement edged to an attack on the very assumptions of imperialism. What was once invisible about imperialism became visible and costly. When Nixon came to the Presidency, he realized that to save the principles and the apparatus of imperialism he had to stop the involvement of the military in a war-fighting role.

As we have seen, a person who wants to be recognized as a great President must be active. He will come to power wanting to *do* something. He comes to power with imperial pretensions: "I will not lose China," "We will be first," etc. He attempts to control the bureaucracy. He finds that the easiest place to do so is in the national security area where he is the prime constituent of the various agencies and departments. Yet even in national security the question is whether the President will follow the bureaucracy and the military direction or will lead them. The customs, regulations, and orders of the government that cannot be traced directly to public discussion or congressional intention (para-law) are developed in two different ways. One flow is from the bureaucracy to the President; the other from the President to the bureaucracy. In internal security affairs, the bureaucracies attempt to coopt the President to their purpose. He is to be manipulated to reflect and protect their own internal hierarchies of power and purpose.*

In the period since Kennedy, White House officials attempted to control and develop their own para-legal statements through the National Security Council and the Office of Management and Budget. These presidential agencies set up internal committees in the government to establish policies for the President to take and structure situations which leave the White

---

* In the battle for paramountcy between the various agencies the President's authority is sought as a means to legitimate a particular action or direction. Executive orders, answers to hypothetical questions for press conferences, orders and proclamations are supplied to the President and the executive offices for signature or public affirmation. Such documents or "language," as it is called, are of importance in determining the relative strength of one agency over another.

House various alternatives. Prior to the Bay of Pigs, national security policy generated from the departments of government rather than the White House. Thus, as a rule, covert operations were activities generated by the bureaucracy. Unless a specific order not to go ahead was pronounced by the White House, the agency would carry out its imperial thrust unhampered by presidential involvement. Paradoxically, by trying to stop certain covert operations, the President and his staff were coopted into the demonic work of the national security bureaucracy.

"During the cold war period, the president and his immediate entourage became, in effect, the brokers for the illegitimate power wielded by such agencies as the CIA and the NSA. *Ad hoc* committees threaded the lines between legitimacy and illegitimacy." [7] Much of the time of the President was spent stopping the excesses of uniformed and un-uniformed officials. After the failure at the Bay of Pigs of the CIA, President Kennedy, Robert Kennedy, and McGeorge Bundy undertook to control the national security bureaucracy through presidentially appointed committees dominated by the White House. This "reform" more deeply implicated the Presidency in paramilitary and criminal affairs.

Nixon believed that initiative in national security should emanate from him and his immediate staff. The national security state structure was drowning in the swamps of Indochina. But to save the state, he had to exert himself as the leader *against* the bureaucracies. He could not use the State Department to negotiate the end of the Indochina war or a changed policy toward China. He could no longer trust such agencies as the FBI and the CIA. Therefore, he established in the White House his own special force of operators who would allow maximum flexibility in economics, covert operations, and diplomatic initiatives. The very phrase "maximum flexibility" gave rise to a new stage, the leader-commander stage, and a new form of law. "Maximum flexibility" meant in practice that the control techniques which cold-war Presidents and the bureaucracy had sanctioned against the poor and the "subversives" at home, and which had been transported abroad, were again brought home to be used against the middle classes and the bureaucracies themselves, and even against leaders of the two major political parties.

Stage III: Leader-Commander State— Law by Whim and Command

In both class law and para-law there exists a framework of commonly understood actions and likely directions which the bureaucracy or the corporations will take. However, once a serious economic disaster or failed war occurs, a new stage is reached. At this point, an attempt will be made to assert tyrannical leadership wherein an individual and his retinue will make ad hoc decisions that are arbitrarily determined by each separate case or whim. This has been the experience of other executive governments with a strong military and corporate elite. In Germany, during Hitler's time, "a strong government unhampered by individual persons, groups, classes, estates, parties and parliament" was the goal of Nazi leadership.[8] In the period of the leader, maximum emphasis is placed on flexibility for leadership. No obvious peaceful controls can be exercised either by the bureaucracies, the barons, different institutions such as churches, or the people.

The modern tyrant, let us call him the commander, expects to act and execute; deliberation is no longer crucial. He is not to dither, like Adlai Stevenson or a parliamentary socialist party. "Crises" demand an end to dithering from its leader. The President is supposed to decide and react within minutes as to whether or not he should order the world destroyed. This was a prerogative given to him by technology, former Presidents, and the bureaucracy. He also may order spot invasions, as Nixon did in Cambodia and Johnson did in the Dominican Republic. Nixon has appreciated this power given him by his predecessors. He intended to pass on this gift to others. The barons and all presidential aspirants believe that such power is needed to perpetuate the System. They do not see such power as the very reflection of tyranny.

Benito Mussolini once remarked that the twentieth century was the century of the state and command. But more likely, the twentieth century is the last hurrah of such hierarchic, automatic control from the top. If this conjecture is correct, this is a dangerous period for the American people. The state bureaucracy lashes about like a fish out of water trying to generate its own rules and purposes while political leaders, military commanders, and others come forward hoping to organize sovereign power for themselves, using bureaucratic and corporate institutions which themselves know no limits of behavior.

The result is an even more frightening structure as state power is organized more subtly to fill all the public and private spaces against the people. The state and corporate institutions become the structure to replace the community. As Richard Nixon said, "The spirit has usually been willing. It is the structure that has been weak." [9] What Nixon is describing, of course, is a system of governance from the top (whether state socialist or capitalist) which will allow the dance of the leaders to go on with no control or participation from the people. The latter are trapped like spectators in a theater of the absurd. They do not know how to manifest their own sensibility in purposive, nonsymbolic politics. Instead, they are expected to play-act, namely, vote and attend meetings. They are denied the spaces for moral public action which would prohibit obviously mad, pathological, or criminal behavior of the "players" or the pathological roles and functions of institutions.

Is there any way for the people to climb out of the theater cave of the absurd? Can we leave the three overlapping stages and enter a new one? Millions of people have sought liberation and direct participation. We have witnessed the emergence of workers councils from revolution, and soldiers councils from lost wars in which the officer corps surrendered or ran away; we have seen progressive attempts at the recall of public officials, the election of judges, resolutions in Congress which suggested that the people should decide when the United States should go to war rather than Congress or the Executive. In the last several years, we have seen more attempts at limiting power of the military and government officials, by holding them accountable to the Nuremberg standards, those standards laid on the Axis nations of World War II.

Slogans like "power to the people," "local control," "decentralized authority," and "maximum feasible participation" have been heard from every quarter of the *unorganized*—whether Left, Right, or Center. We have seen attempts in the United States to revive the principle of town meetings and neighborhood governments. Such attempts imply a fundamental question: Will the nations be controlled by the few for the many, by the few for the few, by the many for the many, or the many for the few? In the United States, this question will be deliberated in terms of what power and authority remains with the people as against the state apparatus. Are the people strong enough to confront state and corporate power?

Lewis Mumford wrote, "Urban life had begun in Greece as an animated conversation and had degenerated into a crude agon or physical struggle. Under a succession of royal and imperial conquerors, the conversation ceased—it is the slaves' lot, observed Euripides, 'not to speak one's thought.' With that the struggle likewise came to an end. What was left of the old urban drama was a mere spectacle, a show staged before a passive audience, with professional freaks, contortionists, and dwarfs usurping the place once occupied by self respecting citizens." [10] (It is one of the most ironic side events of this age that the "freaks" are wearing the suits of the citizens, whereas the citizens in the classic sense are often suited up like "freaks.")

In the present American situation, it is crucial to find ways wherein the people, as citizens, can find their tongue and their reason. Otherwise they will be prone to accept every disaster, every excess, and every economic and moral ripoff without comment or confrontation. Even now, there are those in the media who will say that the System successfully worked its will in the Watergate/Nixon affair, and there are those in the bureaucracy and the banks, the corporations and the military, who will bathe themselves in self-congratulation because Nixon's excesses were condemned. They will say that the national security groups, the CIA, the Department of Defense, and the policing agencies—the established power in the bureaucracy and among the elites— "blew the whistle" on Nixon just as they had done with Joe McCarthy.

We will be taught to forget the integral involvement of Nixon, the barons, and the Democratic party in developing the structure in which these excesses occur. Those who brought us the Indochina war and the arms race, those who invented the body counts and the smart bombs, those who daily act on the principle that the American political economy should starve its own society for private profit, calling corporate imperialism "economic growth," have been able to catch their breath and come forward as men of gravitas and decency. That they did not have to make any sort of public penance for the war is a political and moral travesty. They will say that we should return to the assumptions and rules of para-law, of class law, and the national security state. But Humpty Dumpty should not be put together again.

Is There a Fourth Stage?

By this time it should be clear, or I have failed miserably, that I believe authority, responsibility, and law must be located in the people. The people are credited with natural rights which define their personhood. These flow out of their existential condition as human beings; they can be neither summarized nor taken away. They can be discovered through inquiry and a deeper understanding of ourselves. Such inquiry may be seen as the project of the human sciences. Beyond individual rights, people fashion additional legal, economic, and political rights because they have agreed to be bound and to work together in a community. These rights should be decided not through a complicated system of interest bargaining that has no existential relevance but, to the extent possible, in face-to-face discussion, and then in further dialogue with other communities through assemblies and congresses. The community should find ways to discuss what they will *not* do under any circumstances to others. Thus, they may give up "ultimate" weapons and imperial wars as their means of protection because they know that otherwise they will cease to be a community and people will become instead individuated pawns in the game of power with nuclear props and imperial purposes. *Finally, the communities, perhaps at the insistence of radical reconstruction democrats should develop minimum levels of well-being which must be maintained (because they undercut humanity if they are not maintained) before any inequality can be countenanced, notwithstanding the fact that inequality already exists in practice.*

It is one of the conceits of the twentieth century to believe that this idea stems from modern revolutions. Students of the medieval period know better. The first task for a community is to decide the minimum. In the Middle Ages, according to Kropotkin, this minimum was guaranteed before there was a market. Food and lodging were produced and built which guaranteed enough to everyone in the community. It was at this point that a market was allowed to come into being. Kropotkin points out some of the leading ideas of the eleventh century which are not irrelevant to the transformation of our own political system.

> Self reliance and federalism, the sovereignty of each group and the construction of the political body from the simple to the composite, were the leading ideas of the eleventh century. But since that time the conceptions had entirely changed. The students of Roman law and the prelates of the Church, closely bound together since the time of Innocent the Third, had succeeded in paralyzing the idea—the antique Greek idea—which presided at the foundation of the cities. For two or three hundred years they taught from the pulpit, the University chair, and the judges' bench that salvation must be sought for in a strongly centralized state, placed under a semi-divine authority; that one man can and must be the savior of society, and that in the name of salvation he can commit any violence, burn men and women at the stake, make them perish under indescribable tortures, plunge whole provinces into the most abject misery. Nor did they fail to give object lessons to this effect on a grand scale, and with an unheard of cruelty, wherever the king's sword and the Church's fire, or both at once, could reach. By these teachings and example, continually repeated and enforced upon public attention, the very minds of the citizens had been shaped into a new mould. They began to find no authority too extensive, no killing by degrees too cruel, conceit was for the "public safety." [11]

While it is beyond the scope of these Notes to discuss the relationship of the American side of the Enlightenment to Kropotkin's views of the city and the guilds, suffice it to say that the American Revolution was not closed to such perceptions. Indeed, the American Revolution attempted to open a new definition of humanity and a long-term historical process leading to the political principle that energy and sovereignty rests with the people, neither with a President nor a state, not with the Joint Chiefs of Staff or General Motors, not a political party, or even a Congress denuded of relationship to the people. This view of the American system has not been realized.

7 / Law and the People

Alfred De Grazia has pointed out that the eighteenth-century Congress "was the product of the Enlightenment Mind and of the political forces born of that mind. It contained in its design several distinctive principles. First of all, the legislature should be the First Branch of Government. It should have the supreme power to legislate and to intervene in the government whenever and wherever individuals were done injustice." [1] But, as De Grazia goes on to say, the word "mass" was missing from the vocabulary of the eighteenth century. The Founding Fathers still thought of the masses as the mob; today's rulers continue to see the people through such a distorted lens. The American Congress has this difficulty. During the period of antiwar marches in Washington it was not until 1971 that members of Congress would see the marchers as anything but a mob. Members of Congress were frightened by the marches; most identified their interests with state power, the military (almost 100 of them retain, illegally, commissions in the military), and the Presidency. Yet, in the marchers' eyes, Congress was viewed as a possible instrument of the people. And there is political sense to this perspective.

Without Congress, the people and the citizenry would be totally at the mercy of executive bureaucracy, the corporations, the military, and the police. There would be no place to register dissent or to exercise any sort of restraint over the powerful and their headless, soulless institutions. At this point, the dour reader will most likely think that *this is* the case at present, even though Congress exists. The reader would be correct—unless Congress and the people find a way to alter the relationship of Congress to the citizenry. Unless Congress seeks its legitimacy in the people through an increasing unity with them, it will be consigned to begging its daily operating legitimacy from the corporations, the military, and the bureaucracy.

In this section of the Notes, I discuss in a cursory fashion a way to develop a new ongoing relationship between Congress and the people. Needless to say, we must be very careful in recommending any sort of legal "reform." A reform in and of itself may appear to be useful and wise, although in a larger political framework it may turn out to be quite regressive because it reinforces the power of the leader, oligarchs, and the repressive apparatus. It thus perpetuated a quality of autism among the people.

Questions that are now hidden by masks and structural madness need to be debated openly and understood so that they will not be mediated through indirect manipulation and private deals. Once the debate is open and the issues understood, we may expect profound changes in the purpose of the American state. It is likely that MIRV, for example, would be voted down if it were to be debated and voted on in town meetings or grand juries in the congressional districts. Its development would be seen as mad and its use criminal. If citizens would vote on the programs of the federal budget or on paying their taxes locally, it seems doubtful that an imperial war budget (the kind the United States has) would be chosen over a defense budget or a series of creative plans for urban and town reconstruction. It is hard to imagine that a majority of the citizenry, after their own inquiry and serious discussion in their places of work and in their precincts, would favor the present income, wealth, and land distribution. They would object not only because of the obvious inequity, but also because such inequity undercuts the possiblity of achieving a democratic body politic and a quality of humanness which is present but dormant. This humane quality would be awakened through public discussion and deliberation.

Many ideas, if tried, would return power to the people. But any proposal must now have several objectives. It cannot have vague purposes, yet it must be sufficiently open as a structural mechanism to contemplate profound changes and facilitate their occurrence. It must, to the extent possible, build on the natural good sense of the people who may appear colonized only because they have not found a way to act. It must have a spiritual component which binds people to one another, as well as procedures that allow each to be heard by all.

I do not doubt the validity of substantive proposals that would have far-reaching consequences. Rather, I think their validity must be discussed in a context of local deliberation and participation by the people. For example, one staple of militarism, and a centralized bureaucracy which feeds that militarism, is the withholding tax system—a system of taxation that, when first put into effect in the early 1940s, was said to be "temporary" by both political parties. There is no reason why, in a federal system, workers should not control their taxes until the end of a year, and then decide to what political and legal authority their taxes should be paid. There is no reason, for example, why national budgets could not be voted locally in assemblies, or why the people should not demand that the largest corporations begin a transformation toward control by communities of workers and consumers. There is no reason why the world's cities cannot exchange compacts of friendship with one another. But these and other matters must be contemplated and debated by the people through institutions that will allow the maximum amount of wisdom to come forward.

As I have said, Congress can find its legitimacy by opening a dialogue with the people. Only through dialogue, inquiry, and deliberation can a modern political system with any pretense to freedom be sustained or transformed without a continuous civil war. For this purpose, therefore, it becomes crucial to apply institutional forms which have general acceptance. People would feel the most comfortable with such forms, and could then use them to transform the alienated and discredited politics of the executive institutions. One such form is the *grand jury*.

Historically the grand jury served two purposes. The first, and the one most familiar to us, is the jury's power of deliberation and decision as to whether or not to bring an individual to trial. Indictments were developed through information brought to the grand jury by the Crown prosecutor, although apparently the grand juries could act on their own knowledge, as a result of their own investigations. This latter method, the presentment, allowed the English grand juries to "investigate any matter that appeared to them to involve a violation of the law." [2] In the last several years this form of the grand jury has played an extraordinary and complex role. Grand juries have thwarted prosecutors who have attempted to bring cases against antiwar movement leaders; a grand jury has named President Nixon as an unindicted co-conspirator. Yet grand juries have also acted as a rubber stamp for the office of the prosecutor. For example, the Department of Justice under John Mitchell's leadership used the grand jury as a mechanism for state repression and surveillance, suggesting the dangerous turn that the modern grand jury mechanism can take.

From its inception in the United States, however, the grand jury had a second form and purpose. According to Younger, the grand jury "played an important role in America and became a vital force in local government. . . . Grand juries acted in the nature of local assemblies: making known the wishes of the people, proposing new laws, protesting against abuses in government, performing administrative tasks and looking after the welfare of their communities." Established forces of the society, however, worked "diligently to overthrow the institution. And where the grand jury was emasculated or abolished, the power and authority of judges and prosecutors was increased." [3]

In the American prerevolutionary period, the grand jury played an important role in discovering and defining the life of the community. It received its power either from the town meeting (as in Massachusetts) or from the county court (as in Virginia) to investigate violations of the law and poor public policy. Its form of inquiry served a powerful social role which assumed that learning, moral instruction, and education took place in the public space, meaning that it was the responsibility of the people acting as citizens. The grand jury investigated wife beating in Massachusetts, rebuked the town of Sandwich "for not having their swine ringed," and questioned the arrangements of the governor and his assistants to sell lands to certain people. In Connecticut the grand juries were to make sure that the children of the colony learned to read. Each juryman was ordered "to visit families in his town whom he suspected of neglecting the order to teach all children to read." In Virginia the grand jury set the price of private property, reported on the roads and building conditions, etc., and "checked upon those who failed to attend church on Sunday." [4]

The growth of the colonial towns saw the development of the grand jury as "an instrument for popular participation in municipal as well as county and provincial government." [5] They were the means whereby citizens exercised deliberative and executory functions. Because the grand jury became a weapon against tyranny and economic power, the British trustees—absentee landlords—tried to limit the power of the grand juries to narrow questions put before them by judges. But grand juries were hard to control. They led the opposition to the British Crown during the revolutionary period and sought ways to fashion their own oaths. They refused to indict the leaders of the Stamp Act riots and refused to be intimidated by the royal judges who demanded indictments against those who wrote "libelous" material denouncing the quartering of royal troops. In New York the jurors issued a protest in 1775 against "the many oppressive acts of Parliament," and in South Carolina grand jurors drafted a "veritable Declaration of Independence." [6] The grand jury was thus an instrument for the development of the Constitution. But, in saying this, it should be recalled that the Constitution was a profoundly bourgeois document—whether one is a Hamiltonian or a Jeffersonian. Consequently, while it guaranteed rights of freemen, it conferred citizenship—powers of deliberation and decision— only to the few.

Thus, in prerevolutionary America, the grand jury was used to find out the problems of government and to institutionalize citizen control and participation. If it were now employed as part of Congress, the grand jury could open the way to the emergence of a participatory nation in which citizenship would become the linchpin of a modern American democracy. My hope is that the people and Congress (assuming its interest in attaching itself to the people) would serve as an offensive check against the executive state which grounds its legitimacy in creatures of its own invention—namely, the corporation, the military, and the bureaucracy.

Congress needs to relate directly to the people without passing through the administrative hands of the executive. This is necessary so that we may find out, discover the condition of the people, the citizenry, and the institutions. This can be done through a national grievance procedure, perhaps a national grievance day, in which discussions and town meetings are held in the districts by congressmen. People will discover a sense of who they are, a sense of themselves as participants, and a response to their real needs outside the framework of abstract interests. They will begin to see one another. From such town meetings, Congress could establish a permanent congressional grand jury system in the districts to investigate the major public institutions and to encourage open town meetings with agendas which would address the content and direction of governing in the districts, the nature and structure of baronial and state power. Such an institutional arrangement can be seen as a way of protecting the legitimacy of the Constitution and providing the Congress with the power to confront the Executive. For example, there is no way to have an impeachment and conviction of a President without the direct involvement of the people. On the other hand, if the people are integrated with the legislative process, executive tyranny, the fear of the eighteenth-century Founding Fathers and philosophers, will be obviated.

The pattern of inquiry that the congressional grand juries would pursue could cause the removal of the barriers that various elites, the synthetic national personalities, have put between the people and what needs to be known, understood, and acted upon by the citizenry. Their primary stated task would be to develop the ideas and programs of the citizens. Congressional grand juries would point out and debate the major institutional crises in forums of investigation which would stimulate the consciousness of the people. Once their justifiable paranoia is vented, people may begin to express a quality of empathy, fairness, and inquiry which is now shackled in the private, isolated lives of individuals. Participatory citizenship may be the means for the removal of the shackles of lonely, anomic people and for the reassertion of sovereignty in themselves. Through the process of the congressional grand jury and the development of local assemblies, people will discover themselves in their existential sense and will be empowered to define the meaning of their citizenship in a political and active way.

> Though something of righteousness may become evident in the life of the individual, righteousness itself can only become wholly visible in the structures of the life of a people. These structures enable righteousness to be realized, functioning internally within the various groups of the people, and externally in the people's relations to other nations; to function in abundance and diversity and with regard to all possible social, political, and historical situations. Only life can demonstrate the absolute, and it must be the life of the people as a whole.[7]

There is another purpose of the grand jury which is less spiritual, having to do with the control and dismantling of the machinery of state violence. Congress and the people must find ways of relating to each other continuously so that responsible constitutional control over the armed forces will be exercised. The armed forces and paramilitary groups control the fate of nations and peoples today. They control the fate of republics and democracies as Allende, the French Assembly in the Fourth Republic, south Asian, Latin American, and African governments have all learned. For the United States, the question is whether there can be a relationship between Congress and the American people so that the armed forces will see their allegiance to the Constitution and the people rather than to themselves or a President who has criminal or imperial intentions. If the officer corps of the armed forces do not have allegiance to the people and the Constitution, there will be no way in which Congress and the citizenry can withstand an armed takeover or an armed takeover by erosion (through the national security state and the budget).[8]

The grand jury proposal should be judged by the reader in the context of its history and in the context of our own time. Those familiar with its past will know that it has served narrow interests. Before the American Revolution, the southern colonies used the grand jury to defend the institution of slavery and the property rights of the new bourgeois class against the king and his trustees. Yet their struggle had, for that time, important progressive elements because it was a force for decolonization against the king of England. History has also taught that the king of England and his trustees were not antislavery. The British Empire countenanced slavery abroad well into the twentieth century and so, of course, had supported the South's. After the revolution, grand juries also served the bourgeois class which felt threatened by Shay's Rebellion. That event was a major and immediate reason for the Constitutional Convention. The Massachusetts legislature suspended the writ of habeas corpus and sent troops to crush the opposition. The juries were powerless and acted out of their own class interests. They were unable to test the complaints of the rebels and to grant them economic relief.

But today, during this period, there is a different feeling within the United States. It is generally accepted by the people that institutions and laws are used against them rather than for them and that the System is rapidly detaching itself from the people. Obviously, the grand jury will not be the same throughout the United States. It is likely, however, that it will give space for people, in whatever region, to come forward and translate their hope into the will to change their institutions.

Political mechanisms such as the grand jury may help people to "see clearly" what is going on and then "problematically" to offer suggestions and alternatives that will allow their own humanity to be mediated through their own citizenship beyond class. It will be through public inquiry and deliberation that people will see each other beyond class, reaching out while disentangling each other from roles and structures that have to be shaken and transformed.

The contours of the congressional grand jury I propose might be developed along the following lines:

1. Congressional juries would be chosen from expanded jury lists in each congressional district. Every person eighteen years of age and older would be eligible. There would be no property, sex, religion, or race qualifications. Those who had served terms in prison for misdemeanors or felonies would be eligible once their terms of confinement in prison ended.

2. Government civil servants would be eligible without loss of civil service benefits.

3. Congressional grand juries would have the power to investigate all questions within a particular district which have come before the Congress through legislation or hearings, bills, or prolonged debate. The congressional jury would also be empowered to initiate issues it considers important for Congress to know about. They would have the power to investigate the operations of corporations doing business in their district. They would have the power to hold hearings; point out abuses; recommend changes, new legislation, and programs. In general, they could take testimony, hold hearings, and propose legislation on all areas that directly or indirectly affect the citizen, including defense and national security policy, income and wealth problems, land reform, ecology, rights guaranteed under the Constitution, and revision of the laws.

4. The congressional grand jury would have a continuing mandate to develop means for full participatory citizenship of the people as guaranteed in Articles 9 and 10 of the Constitution. It would develop ongoing local assemblies of the people to deliberate on all questions of national, transnational, and local concern.

5. *Each member of Congress, depending on the number of people in his or her district, would have at least one jury for every 50,000 residents.*

6. *Each jury would have 24 members, elect its own chairman, and develop its own internal governing procedures consistent with procedures promulgated by both houses of Congress. All hearings would be open to the public and to the media.*

7. *Members of the congressional grand jury would serve for only two years, and the congressional juror would be excused from any further service after having served one term.*

8. *Grand jury reports would be made public in each congressional district. They would be filed regularly with the member of Congress in whose district the grand jury is located, and would be circulated through the local schools for comment and discussion among students and teachers.*

9. *The grand juries would not have presentment power, nor would they have the power to indict.*

10. *Congressional members of each state would meet for a one-week period at the end of each session of Congress with the congressional grand jurors to review their recommendations, investigations, and suggested legislation.*

11. *A deputy clerk of the House would be appointed for congressional grand juries to perform those duties assigned by the Congress.*

In this proposal, I do not want to be understood as meaning that the citizenry must wait for Congress to act. It is the people, in their role as citizens, who can fill the spaces of politics, once the people become aware of the need for such action. Their actions do not have to wait for structural changes. Their impulse for action comes from understanding their needs through struggle, decolonization, inquiry, and reaching out to others like themselves. At first, they trade their needs, seeing in one another their own humanity and therefore the project for further action. It is a process of political action which stems from a spirit, a need which transcends the particular moment or problem to develop a community that asserts the person as part of the community, while protecting him from it.

Translated into the present context, people can organize one another through town meetings, a structure of venting that starts the dialogic process of what needs to be done. Hannah Arendt has said that the polis is "the space of men's free deeds and living words [which] could endow life with splendor." [9] But we know now that such splendor is beyond us unless we can find ways of recovering our own humanity, self-evident, invariant, and undeniable, while finding means of tactically surviving by transforming institutions of deliberation and making them the *instruments of the people as people and as citizens.*

Americans are fortunate in their Constitution. Now we should learn to use it. The neglected and undefined Ninth Amendment, for example, states, "The enumeration in the Constitution of certain rights shall not be construed to deny or otherwise disparage others retained by the people." Surely those rights are more than the right to privacy. The eighteenth-century American Enlightenment *philosophes* believed in inherent rights which no constitution or government could barter away. The modern age started from this principle. Its symbol, the Declaration of Independence, had said that there were self-evident inalienable rights "such as life, liberty and the pursuit of happiness." The phrase "such as" meant that natural rights were not a fixed category that could be spelled out or laid down for time immemorial. It was an *expanding* category as people discovered their needs and discovered themselves. They disdained the institutional epaulets of pomp and power which hid people from one another. In our time, faulty superstructures are again hiding us from each other. Our synthetic creations, the corporations and the state, now claim that they grant us our inalienable rights. How

amusing this would seem to the eighteenth-century revolutionary. But we cannot be amused. There is no room for amusement
now because the question of what is inalienable goes to the very
core of human *being* and survival.

No doubt there will be objections about raising this question
at the end of this essay. What can Congress and grand juries do
for the people and their rights on such grave questions? First, we
must see these forms as the people's instruments and, second,
they must become the connecting link to a new system which
starts and ends with the people. Third, we are required to reject
the politics of sham, play acting, and interest bartering, defining
instead a politics that can reflect our own humanity in our own
structure, taking our own risks. Our task is to set the foundations
for a new stage, using what is at hand to build, requiring that we
speak and act for ourselves, but with one another.

Notes

Notes

Chapter 1.
The President's Burlesque and His Bank of Political Power

1. Letter to Helen H. Taft, 8 July 1894, quoted in Carl Solberg, *Riding High: America in the Cold War* (New York: Mason & Lipscomb, 1973), p. 30; also in Henry F. Pringle, *The Life and Times of William Howard Taft,* II (New York: Farrar & Rinehart, 1939).

2. Rear Admiral Donald T. Poe, "Command and Control: Changeless Yet Changing" (Strategic Research Group: National War College, 1973), p. 2

3. Edmund Wilson, *Patriotic Gore: Studies in the Literature of the American Civil War* (New York: Oxford University Press, 1966), pp. xiv-xv. Letter to Senator James Hammond of South Carolina from William Simms.

/162/

4. Hans J. Morgenthau, *The Purpose of American Politics* (New York: Alfred A. Knopf, 1960), p. 274.

5. Antonio Gramsci, *Prison Notebooks: Selections*, ed. Quinton Hoare and Geoffrey N. Smith (New York: International Publishers), p. 129.

6. Paul Sweezy and Leo Huberman, "The Kennedy-Johnson Boom," in *The Great Society Reader: The Failure of American Liberalism*, ed. Marvin E. Gettleman and David Mermelstein (New York: Vintage Books, 1967), p. 102.

7. Theodore Roosevelt, *Autobiography* (1914), p. 24.

8. William Letwin, "On Development of Capitalism," *Daedalus* 99 (1970): 14.

9. Henry A. Wallace, *Whose Constitution* (New York: Reynal & Hitchcock, 1936), pp. 153-75.

10. Sidney Fine, *Laissez Faire and the General Welfare State* (Ann Arbor: University of Michigan Press, 1964), p. 214. Analysis and quotation from the platform of the Society for the Study of National Economy written by Nelson Patten and Edmund J. James.

11. Fine, *Laissez Faire*, pp. 221-26.

12. Wallace, *Whose Constitution*, pp. 156-57.

13. Ibid., p. 170.

14. Samuel R. Reid, *Mergers, Managers and the Economy* (New York: McGraw-Hill, 1968), pp. 73, 128.

15. Alexander Hamilton, *The Federalist No. 31* (New York: Mentor Books, 1961), p. 194.

16. Anne O'Hare McCormick, "The New Ordeal of Democracy," in *The New Deal*, ed. Carl Degler (New York: Quadrangle Books, 1970), pp. 37-38.

17. Opening statement of Senator Frank Church before the Special Committee on the Termination of the National Emergency of the U.S. Senate (11 April 1973), p. 1.

18. Emergency Power Statutes Report of the Special Committee on the Termination of the National Emergency (U.S. Senate), p. 7.

19. *Youngstown Sheet and Tube* v. *Sawyer*, 343 U.S. 579 (1952).

20. Ibid.

21. *Mississippi* v. *Johnson*, 4 Wall. 475 (U.S. 1867).

22. *Marbury* v. *Madison*, 1 Cranch 137 (U.S. 1803).

23. Edward Corwin, *President: Office & Powers* (4th ed.; New York: New York University Press, 1957).

24. Richard J. Barnet, *Roots of War* (New York: Pelican Books, 1973), pp. 95–137.

25. Testimony of John D. Ehrlichman before the Senate Select Committee on Presidential Campaign Activities of 1972, vol. 7, 25 June 1973.

Chapter 2.
Nixon Before the Storm: Supreme Survivor and Master Politician

1. Gaetano Mosca, *The Ruling Class* (New York: McGraw-Hill, 1939), p. 203.

2. Machiavelli, "Discorsi I," in *The Prince and the Discourses*, ed. Sergio Bertelli (Milan: Feltrinelli, 1960), p. xxv.

3. Richard M. Nixon, *Six Crises* (Garden City, N.Y.: Doubleday, 1962).

4. Richard M. Nixon, "Plans for the Second Term," 27 November 1972.

5. Ibid.

6. Nixon campaign speech, 30 October 1972.

7. Spiro T. Agnew, Speech at the Pennsylvania Republican Dinner, Harrisburg, Pa., 30 October 1969.

8. Spiro T. Agnew, Speech at the National Governors' Conference, Washington, D.C., 26 February 1973.

9. Research paper of Bethany Weidner, Institute for Policy Studies (1972); analysis of Vice-President Spiro Agnew's speech, p. 20.

10. Richard M. Nixon, Speech at John Connally's Picosa Ranch, Floresville, Texas, 22 September 1972.

11. Ibid.

12. Richard M. Nixon, referred to later in Speech before the Business Executives Club of Chicago, Ill., 17 March 1955.

13. See Henry Kissinger, *Nuclear Weapons and Foreign Policy* (New York: Harper & Bros. for the Council on Foreign Relations, 1957), in which he advocates the use of tactical nuclear weapons.

14. Richard M. Nixon, Radio Address on defense policy, 29 October 1972.

15. Quoted in Earl Ravenal, "The Nixon Doctrine—Defense Policy and China," *Peace With China? U.S. Decisions for Asia,* ed. Earl Ravenal (New York: Liveright, 1971), pp. 28-29.

16. Secretary of State William Rogers' statement on War Powers Legislation in hearings before the Subcommittee on National Security Policy and Scientific Developments, Committee on Foreign Affairs of the House of Representatives (June 1971), p. 127.

17. "Interview with Jeb Stuart Magruder," *Harper's Magazine,* October 1973.

18. Theodore White, *The Making of the President 1972* (New York: Atheneum, 1973), p. 303.

19. Rosa Luxemburg, *The Accumulation of Capital* (New York: Modern Reader, 1968), pp. 447-48.

20. Hearings on the Operations of Multinational Corporations, Senate Foreign Relations Committee, March 1973, pp. 93 ff.

21. David Carper, "Moral Dave Beck—Unethical Scapegoat," in *Voices of Dissent,* ed. Irving Howe (New York: Grove Press, 1958), p. 161.

22. Hearings on Organized Crime—Securities: Thefts and Frauds, the Permanent Subcommittee on Investigations, vols. 1-3, October 1973.

23. Quoted in unpublished paper by Stephen Rosenfeld, "The Riddle of James Schlesinger" (June 1974), p. 4.

24. James Madison, *The Federalist, No. 10* (New York: Mentor Books), p. 82.

25. William Howard Taft, Lectures on the Presidency delivered at Columbia University, 1915-16. Note discussion in Senate Report No. 93-549. Report of the Special Committee on the Termination of the National Emergency of the United States (U.S. Senate, 19 November 1973).

26. R. M. MacIver, *The Modern State* (New York: Oxford University Press, 1932), p. 199.

27. Richard M. Nixon, Press Conference, 5 October 1972, reprinted in *Weekly Compilation of Presidential Documents,* Fourth Quarter.

28. Richard M. Nixon, Press Conference, 27 November 1972, reprinted in *Weekly Compilation of Presidential Documents,* vol. 8, no. 49, p. 1703.

29. Stephen Liebfried, "U.S. Central Government Reform of the Administrative Structure During the Ash Period (1968-1971)," *Kapitalistate* 1, no. 2 (1973): 17-30.

Chapter 3.
The Passive Branch

1. Joint Hearings before the Ad Hoc Committee on Impoundment of Funds, January 1973 (Senate Government Operations and Judiciary Committee), p. 33.

2. Quoted in Rexford G. Tugwell, *The Enlargement of the Presidency* (Garden City, N.Y.: Doubleday, 1960), pp. 198-206.

3. Conversation with Benjamin V. Cohen, chief draftsman of the lend-lease arrangement with Great Britain.

4. *United States* v. *Midwest Oil Company,* 236 U.S. 459.

5. Secretary of the Treasury Douglas Dillon, Speech delivered at the Harvard Business School, 6 June 1964.

6. Budget Message of the President, 1973.

7. Hearings on Impoundment (Senate Government Operations and Judiciary Committee).

8. 21 Attorney General's Opinions 415 (U.S. 1896).

9. Louis Fisher, "Presidential Spending Discretion and Congressional Controls," *Law and Contemporary Problems* (Winter 1972).

10. Ibid.

11. Hearings on Impoundment (Senate Government Operations and Judiciary Committee).

12. Ibid., p. 361.

13. Ibid., Hearings on S.373 (Senate Government Operations Committee), 16 January 1973, pp. 93–121.

14. Ibid., p. 53.

15. Conference on Congressional Prerogatives, Fund for New Priorities, Washington, D.C., Winter 1973.

16. Lincoln said, "whether strictly legal or not," he moved against the rebellion "under what appeared to be public demand and a public necessity; trusting then as now, that Congress would readily ratify them." Quoted in Executive Document 1, 37th Cong., 1st sess., 9. Also quoted in Rexford Tugwell, *Englargement of the Presidency,* p. 150.

17. Testimony given by E. Howard Hunt to the U.S. Federal Court, Washington, D.C., 1973.

18. *Brown* v. *United States,* 8 Cranch 110 (U.S. 1814).

19. National Emergency Hearings, Special Committee on the National Emergency, 24 July 1973, p. 507.

20. Senator Goldwater listed 199 military operations "which were conducted without any declaration of war." *Congressional Record,* 20 July 1973, pp. S-14174–85.

21. Report 220 of the Senate Foreign Relations Committee, June 1973, p. 2.

22. Ibid., pp. 4-9.

23. Ibid.

24. Remarks by Senator James Abourezk, 20 July 1973, *Congressional Record,* pp. S-14160–62.

25. Act of 5 June 1794 (Ch. 50), 1 Stat. 384.

26. Supplemental views of J. William Fulbright, Report 220, pp. 33-37.

27. Nixon veto message, 29 October 1973, *Weekly Compilation of Presidential Documents*, p. 1286.

28. Ibid.

29. Marcus Raskin, "Erosion of Congressional Responsibility," in Richard Barnet, Marcus Raskin, and Ralph Stavins, *Washington Plans an Aggressive War* (New York: Random House, 1971).

Chapter 4.
Nixon's Watergate

1. Quoted by Marcus Raskin, "From Eisenhower Vultures to Kennedy Hawks," in *The Pentagon Watchers*, ed. Leonard Rodberg and Derek Shearer (New York: Anchor Books, 1970), p. 93.

2. Vice-President Gerald Ford, 7 May 1974.

3. Richard M. Nixon, Speech to the Young Republicans Leadership Conference, 28 February 1974.

4. Hannah Arendt, *On Revolution* (New York: Viking Press, 1963), p. 99.

Chapter 5.
The Impeached System

1. Harry S. Truman, Presidential Proclamation No. 2914, 16 December 1950. Truman's Proclamation of national emergency, still in effect.

2. *Weekly Compilation of Presidental Documents*, vol. 9, no. 37, p. 1106.

3. Testimony of former Justice Tom Clark before the Senate Special Committee on the Termination of the National Emergency, 25 July 1973.

4. John F. Kennedy, *Profiles in Courage* (New York: Harper & Row, 1958).

5. La Wanda Cox and John Cox, *Politics, Principle and Prejudice 1865-1866* (Glencoe, Ill.: Free Press, 1964), p. 210.

6. 2 Hinds 1597 (U.S. 1907).

7. Ibid., pp. 1590 ff.

8. Rexford G. Tugwell, *The Enlargement of the Presidency* (Garden City, N.Y.: Doubleday, 1960), p. 204. Stanton drafted one of the acts of the radical Republicans, the Supplementary Reconstruction Act.

9. Hearings on the Nomination of William E. Colby for director of the CIA, Senate Committee on the Armed Services, 2 July 1972. See testimony of Colby, pp. 2–33.

Chapter 6.
Law and the State

1. Lyndon Johnson, *The Vantage Point: Perspectives of the Presidency, 1963-69* (New York: Popular Library, 1972).

2. Emmett John Hughes, "A White House Taped," *New York Times Magazine,* 9 June 1974, p. 68.

3. Note the twists and turns of the Supreme Court, beginning with the *Slaughterhouse* cases, 16 Wall. 36 (U.S. 1873); *Munn* v. *Illinois,* 94 U.S. 113 (1877). With *Powell* v. *Pennsylvania,* 127 U.S. 678 (1888); *Allgeyer* v. *Louisiana,* 165 U.S. 578 (1897); and *Santa Clara County* v. *Southern Pacific Railroad Co.,* 118 U.S. 394 (1886) the principle of liberty of contract and the term "person" was extended to include corporations. See discussion in Sidney Fine, *Laissez Faire and the General Welfare State* (Ann Arbor: University of Michigan Press, 1964), p. 150.

4. John R. Commons, *Legal Foundations of Capitalism* (Madison, Wisc.: University of Wisconsin Press and Macmillan, 1924), p. 320.

5. Frances Piven and Richard Cloward, *Regulating the Poor: The Functions of Public Welfare* (New York: Vintage Books, 1971).

6. Robert Borosage, "The Making of the National Security

State," in *The Pentagon Watchers*, ed. Leonard Rodberg and Derek Shearer (New York: Anchor Books, 1970), pp. 3–65.

7. Richard Barnet, Marcus Raskin, and Ralph Stavins, *Washington Plans an Aggressive War* (New York: Random House, 1971), p. 270.

8. Franz Neumann, *Behemoth* (New York: Harper Torchbooks, 1944), p. 49.

9. Quoted in Stephen Liebfried, "U.S. Central Government Reform," pp. 17–30.

10. Lewis Mumford, *The City in History* (New York: Harcourt, Brace, 1961), p. 196.

11. Peter Kropotkin, *Mutual Aid* (Boston: Extending Horizons Books, 1914), p. 220.

Chapter 7.
Law and the People

1. Alfred De Grazia, *Congress: The First Branch of Government* (Washington, D.C.: American Enterprise Institute, 1966), p. 2.

2. Richard Younger, *The People's Panel* (Providence, R.I.: Brown University Press, 1963), p. 1. Also W. S. Holdsworth, *A History of English Law* (London, 1903), 1:147–48.

3. Younger, *People's Panel*, p. 2.

4. Ibid., passim, chap. 3, pp. 27–40.

5. Ibid., chap. 4, pp. 41-55; chap. 5, pp. 56-71.

6. Ibid., chap. 2, pp. 5–27.

7. Martin Buber, "The Gods of the Nations and God," in *Israel and the World: Essays in a Time of Crisis* (New York: Schocken Books, 1948).

8. Marcus Raskin, "Governing Through Impeachment," *New York Times,* 25 May 1974.

9. *Hannah Arendt, On Revolution* (New York: Viking Press, 1963), p. 285.

Index

Index